A HISTORY OF DERBYSHIRE

Gateway to Tissington Hall

THE DARWEN COUNTY HISTORY SERIES

A History of Derbyshire

JOY CHILDS

Cartography by **R. Rowell** and **K. Moore**

PHILLIMORE

1987

Published by
PHILLIMORE & CO. LTD.
Shopwyke Hall, Chichester, Sussex

ISBN 0 85033 620 2

Printed in Great Britain by
The University Press, Oxford

Contents

National Park boundary sign

List of Plates

Cork Stone, Stanton Moor

7

List of Maps

The marginal drawings are by the author

Acknowledgements

The ongoing process of Derbyshire's history is frequently the subject of specialised and detailed studies, which continue to shed new light on the many different facets of its past. Within limited space, this volume serves as an introductory journey throughout that remarkable history and due reference is made in the Bibliography to the works of writers past and present whose assistance is gratefully acknowledged.

The task of writing and illustrating a volume such as this has been a great challenge and has benefited too from much teamwork, for which special thanks are owed, first and foremost, to my husband Rob for his unstinting belief in this project and endless patience in taking the many photographs he has contributed; to Shane and other family members and friends whose good company was invaluable during the hours of traipsing about with us; to Ruth Rowell and Kate Moore for transforming my laboriously compiled maps into finished artwork; and to Tessa Meetham for contributing four portrait drawings and the illustration of Old Glossop.

Amongst the many people who have generously given their time to pass on snippets of local knowledge, suggest interesting new avenues of approach and above all, deal with the inevitably numerous enquiries generated by complex illustration and writing research, I am particularly grateful to staff of the Derbyshire Libraries, Museums and Information Services, Sheffield City Museum, Leicester University Library, the Peak National Park Joint Planning Board and Repton School.

I am much indebted also with regard to the following:

Drawings; Pin Hole Cave engravings and Creswellian blade in Chapter I reproduced by kind permission of Dr. R. D. S. Jenkinson from *British Archaeological Reports, No. 122 Creswell Crags: Late Pleistocene Sites in the East Midlands* (1984).

Maps; 3 and 4 reproduced from A. E. and E. M. Dodd, *Peakland Roads and Trackways* (2nd edition, 1980), Moorland Publishing Co. Ltd.; 15 reproduced by permission of the Peak National Park Joint Planning Board.

Photographs; No. 2 reproduced by permission of the Cambridge University Collection, copyright reserved; No. 5 courtesy of Sheffield City

Museums; No. 7 by Tessa Meetham; No. 47 printed with the kind permission of Severn-Trent Water Authority, Derwent Division; Nos. 4, 12, 13, 15, 17, 19, 21b, 22, 26, 27, 30, 31, 32, 33, 34, 36, 37, 43, 48, 51, 54, 55 & 56 by Frank Rodgers; Nos. 21a and 35a by Philip Harris.

Chesterfield church

Preface

The beauty of Derbyshire stirred Lord Byron to remark that there are views within the county 'as noble as any in Greece or Switzerland', and, amongst other writers, the philosopher Thomas Hobbes to extol *The Wonders of the Peak*. Yet the ascent into Peakland north of Ashbourne, interspersed with 'grey stone walls . . . and wide-scattered grey stone houses on broken lands where mines had been and were no longer' left the main character in George Eliot's first novel *Adam Bede* singularly unimpressed: 'A hungry land', he declared, 'I'd rather go south'ard where they say it's as flat as a table than come to live here'!

Derbyshire's distinctive shape has been likened to that of a heart, seemingly appropriate to its position in the centre of England. But it is a county centred too on the great natural divide separating Highland and Lowland Britain, for within that heart-shape the upland region of the north-west forms part of the Southern Pennines, while the lowlands to the south and east belong to the valley of the Trent and the Midland Plain. Between highland and lowland there are also marked differences in climate, with colder temperatures and heavier rainfall making the northernmost heights of Kinder Scout and Bleaklow as bleak as the latter's name suggests. These peaty moors, possibly wilder now and even more inhospitable towards human settlement than they were in ancient times, rise over two thousand feet inside the Dark Peak of predominantly gritstone rock, which curves, in an almost encircling horseshoe, around the lighter limestone hills and dales of the White Peak.

The Derbyshire Peak District occupies more than half of Britain's first national park and both its contrasting areas have been and continue to be exploited by man – though they bear far fewer obvious scars than the more populous region of coal measures on the county's eastern side. Even here, however, amid collieries and slag-heaps there are pleasant open spaces, and interest and deceptive beauty lying within its co-existing layers of history. In Tudor times, the ruins of a Norman castle at Bolsover overlooked a 'praty townelet'. Nowadays, a magnificent 17th-century castle oversees an industrial landscape reminiscent of L. S. Lowry paintings, but, when viewed from the M1 motorway, the skyline is soon shared with the towers of Elizabethan Hardwick Hall, rising impressively above its country park – this latter feature in itself a creation in response to modern needs. A few miles away, in the north-eastern corner of the county, a second, much smaller area of limestone housed some of the earliest evidence of human life in Derbyshire, as also did river-terraces along the banks of the Trent. Beyond this major river, the fertile green flatness of the south-eastern corner has in its midst a further belt of coal measures.

Diversity of scenery and richness in a variety of natural resources provide the background to the richly contrasting history of a county which is prolific in its folklore and prevailing customs and traditions. Such is Derbyshire's unique character that, as its story unfolds, we shall see how, despite its remoteness until the 18th century, it has made many special contributions to the wider world in architectural, political, industrial and transport history as well as towards archaeology and conservation.

Ninestones Circle, Harthill Moor, looking towards Robin Hood's Stride

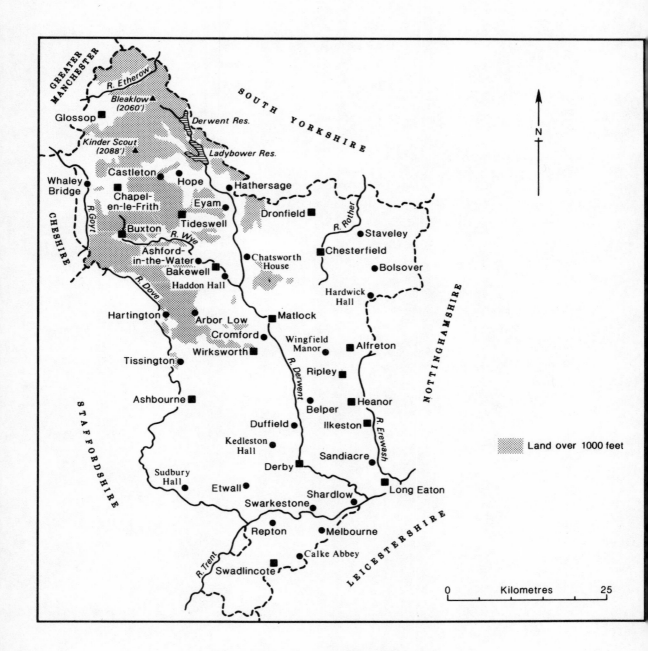

Map 1. The county of contrasts: general map.

16

I Stone and Ice Age

In limestone caves close to Derbyshire's eastern boundary were found the earliest examples of human artistic skill yet known in Britain. These included the figure of a masked man engraved on a piece of bison rib, a fish pattern on a mammoth's tusk, a reindeer rib adorned with a chevron pattern and, oldest of all, a horse's head on another fragment of rib bone. Lethal weapons such as a dagger wrought from a mammoth's spine and utensils, including drinking vessels fashioned from woolly rhinoceros bones, attested further to human ingenuity in the ages long before history was recorded in written form and when daily survival was very much at nature's mercy.

Horse carving, Robin Hood's Cave

The cave-dwellings at Creswell Crags are situated on either side of a narrow gorge sometimes referred to as 'the Cheddar of the North', several feet above its floor, and are remarkable not only for the remains they revealed of occupation by early hunting communities but the timespan, of tens of thousands of years, that intermittent occupation covered – from the middle phase of the Old Stone Age to the first part of the Middle Stone Age. Here, when climatic conditions allowed, the nomadic inhabitants would have found adequate shelter and plentiful supplies of water and food, both from fishing and preying upon the animals which came to drink from the stream. However, evidence of waterlogging inside the caves and variations amongst the numerous species of animal remains pointed to considerable fluctuations in climate, from warm and temperate conditions to arctic. When the first groups took up residence the last advance of the great Ice Age had not yet begun, but by the time the final groups left, the ice had fully retreated and forest growth was once again being established.

Names such as Ashwood Dale in the White Peak recall that forests dominated by ash and hazel formed the natural vegetation of Derbyshire's limestone areas when a temperate climate prevailed. The gritstone moorlands and Trent lowlands were also well wooded, with tree cover of mainly oak and birch similar to that which still graces the slopes of Padley Gorge in north Derbyshire. Amongst the forest fauna, hyenas were the huntsmen's chief rivals in the constant search for meat, but the mild environment supported a rich array for the human diet which included hyenas themselves, deer, bison, wild horses, wild pigs and bears, being further supplemented by the gathering of nuts and berries.

Chevron pattern, Pin Hole Cave

17

The contents of Peakland as well as Creswell caves indicated how that diet changed with the onset of colder conditions preceding an ice advance. Reindeer then provided the most abundant source of food, plus mammoths, woolly rhinoceros, wild cats, wolves, arctic foxes, arctic hares and lemmings. The deterioration in temperatures created an environment of sparse vegetation similar to the tundra of present-day areas such as Siberia. Although the summers were mild, the winters were severe and these conditions also existed immediately after the ice receded. The periods of maximum cold in between, however, when glaciers spread over Derbyshire, forced the migration of its human and animal populations southwards to warmer climes.

Two major ice advances, or glaciations, completely covered the county, but during the last great advance, which ended about 12,000 years ago, there were partial retreats, so enabling hunters and hunted temporarily to return. Derbyshire has fewer traces of the Ice Age than the northern counties, the main effects being the boulder clay deposited in various parts and the presence of rocks known as erratics which were transported by the ice, sometimes over considerable distances from the upland centres of the ice-sheets such as the Lake District, the Cheviots and the Northern Pennines. Glacial deposits occur in the Wye valley from as high as Monsal Dale, but along the Derwent are confined to the area below the confluence of these two rivers, therefore implying that the flow of one glacier from the north-west was along the whole length of the Wye and continued into the southern part of the Derwent. Around Alport in the Wye's tributary valley of Lathkill Dale there are also a few Lake District erratics. But the most important deposits were laid down along the banks of the Trent, where as a result of periodic lowering in the level of the river they have been left in the form of terraces high above the modern floodplain.

Their importance in Derbyshire's history is two-fold, the gravels they contain being now a key natural resource and the discovery of Stone Age tools in them the very first record of people living in the county – indeed, the flint hand-axes found at Hilton have been identified as belonging to the earliest hunters of the Palaeolithic or Old Stone Age. These people flaked a cutting edge along their rough, pear-shaped axes, which were used for scraping as well as the more conventional purposes of chopping and hacking. Other sites, at Willington in the Trent valley and Hopton near Wirksworth, have been associated with hand-axes of later origin than those at Hilton, but even so they are over one hundred thousand years old.

By comparison, the implements associated with the middle Palaeolithic phase are at least thirty thousand years old. From this period came the first evidence of human infiltration into Peakland caves: a flint side-scraper, similar to some of the oldest tools at Creswell Crags, was found at Ravencliffe Cave in the Wye valley. At this time, Neanderthal Man was the dominant human species and roamed the Derbyshire hills in small groups on a transitory basis, following the seasonal migrations

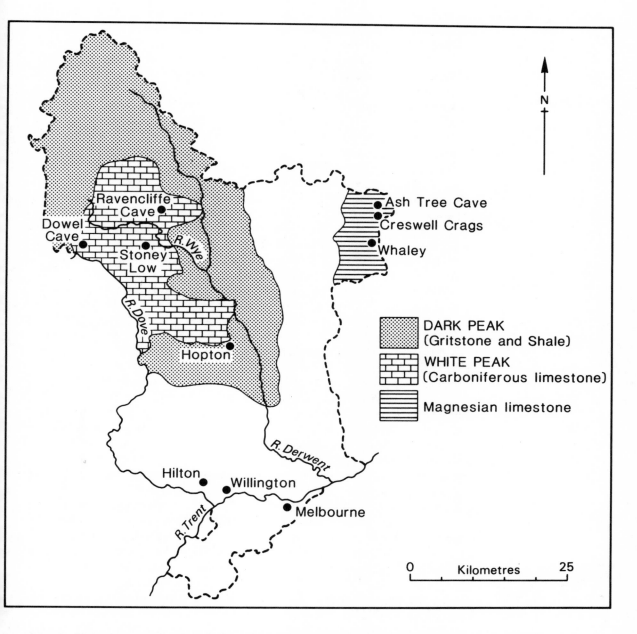

Map 2. Main sites associated with the Old and Middle Stone Ages in highland and lowland Derbyshire.

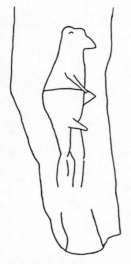

Human figure engraving, Pin Hole Cave

of their prey, especially reindeer. Unlike the finds at Creswell, the zoological remains inside White Peak caves were more rarely the remnants of Stone Age people's meals or particular bones selected for toolmaking. Windy Knoll near Castleton, for instance, seems to have been a shelter for migrating Ice-Age game and also predators, amongst them wolves and grizzly bears.

The Peak District's lack of human interference in the remote past may initially seem surprising, considering the vast cave formations of its limestone area. But surface, life-supporting streams are few in the White Peak, for its Carboniferous limestone rock is extremely porous and more susceptible to the powerful erosive action of water than the geologically younger Magnesian limestone ridge in north-east Derbyshire. Whereas caves including Creswell's inevitably suffered waterlogging when ice melted after glaciations, some Peakland caves could be rendered uninhabitable more frequently by their liability to flood during seasonal changes in the underground water table.

In the endurable spells between glacial cover, the flow of Creswell's surface stream was normally well below the level of the caves. The sequence of occupation began forty to fifty thousand years ago in dwellings which only in the 19th century acquired such fascinating names as Mother Grundy's Parlour, Church Hole, Pin Hole and Robin Hood's Cave. The last two, which are on the northern side of the gorge, contained respectively the bone engravings of the man and the horse, but the time before the production of these rare items was marked by the Neanderthal occupation of the caves and maybe two advances and retreats of the ice-sheets in the last glaciation. Like the horse carving, the representation of the human figure – thought to be wearing an animal mask – was the work of *homo sapiens*, or 'modern' man. Other animal carvings, of a reindeer, a bear or bison's head and a rhino's came from Mother Grundy's Parlour. The heads of these and other large mammals featured significantly too amongst the bones recovered from Creswell. Use as ripping tools has been suggested for lower jaws, with sometimes the powerful canine teeth of bears being removed to serve as smaller cutting tools. Reindeer antlers were also separated from their skulls and, for example in Pin Hole Cave, numbered over a quarter of the 4,400 cranial bones found at various levels in the cave earth. In contrast, the neatly made stone implements there amounted to some two hundred and forty, of which less than a third originated from its earlier residents.

This discrepancy between stone and bone implements hints at the former's lack of ready availability in an inhospitable climate, presumably because ice and snow had more than encroached on the main source of supply. The existence of charcoal with Pin Hole finds provided evidence of fires having been lit, but remains of charred bones from meat being too well-cooked were few. From the need for adaptation to the scarcity of stone grew an inventiveness with bone manifested in such items as the drinking vessels and mammoth spine dagger already mentioned, or

Creswell cave dwelling

even a deadly sword-like weapon which had started out as a woolly rhino's shoulder-blade.

The Neanderthal comings and goings were superseded by the arrival of *homo sapiens* in the area late in the Old Stone Age. A warm interlude ended 27-28,000 years ago and then reoccupation of the caves was not possible until 13-11,000 years ago, at the beginning of the period nowadays termed post-glacial. The gradual improvement in climate was reflected in the predominance of tool-cultures based on finely-worked flint implements – amongst the weapons were spearheads and blades which imply greater competence in methods of hunting. The enterprising inhabitants of Creswell, particularly those in Mother Grundy's Parlour, developed their own local flint 'industry' which has become known in archaeology as the Creswellian culture. Their blades were characteristically small and blunted along one edge for holding or setting into a handle. Creswellian products have also been found as far apart as Somerset caves and several in the White Peak, including Dowel Cave near Earl Sterndale. With its heyday reached before 9500 B.C., this culture continued until after 7000 B.C., so spanning the end of the Old Stone Age and into the second full millennium in the Middle.

Itinerant though life remained for the Middle Stone Age (or Meso-lithic) hunters, there were differences which in their wake brought advantages not hitherto experienced. Firstly, 'man's best friend', the dog, already domesticated thousands of years before its arrival in north-ern Europe in this period, now formed mutually beneficial hunting packs with the human wanderers. Its natural instinct for herding other animals, probably gained from its wolf ancestor which tended to drive prey in herds, was eventually utilised to protect them, extending people's con-trol to previously wild woodland fauna like cattle and pigs. Secondly, their improved weaponry included bows and arrows. Small geometric-ally-shaped flints called microliths were set into resin at the tip of each arrow shaft, but, even this early in its history, the Derbyshire Peak was valued as a source of raw materials, for the inhabitants of the South Pennines favoured a hard black rock called chert from the Wye valley, in addition to flint. Stoney Low, near Ashford-in-the-Water, appears to have been a seasonal centre for hunting, and also making and perhaps trading stone implements. Scatterings of microliths, in association with evidence of hearths, have revealed sites of other temporary Peakland camps, especially on the northern gritstone moors. Although the finds from more southerly sites such as Melbourne showed no use of chert, lowland examples have occurred, for instance in the Magnesian lime-stone caves at Creswell, Ash Tree and Whaley.

Around 5000 B.C. another climatic change brought increased rainfall, and deposits of peat began to blanket the badly-drained gritstone heights of Kinder and Bleaklow, pushing the treeline farther into the valleys. Although at least two thousand years were to pass before people com-menced systematic forest-clearing in other parts of the county, the Derby-shire landscape was starting to assume some of its present-day character.

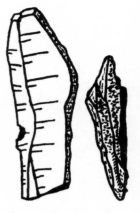

Creswellian flint blade, Pin Hole Cave, and Middle Stone Age micro-lith of Derbyshire chert, Fox Hole Cave near Earl Sterndale

21

II   The Ancient Heritage

'The purposes these places had can only be conjectured', wrote a local 19th-century author called Ebenezer Rhodes concerning ancient sites in the area of Stanton Moor near Birchover. Although archaeology has revealed much information about the people of the New Stone Age and the ensuing Bronze and Iron Ages since his day, his words undoubtedly still hold true and also apply to other Derbyshire remains from these ages, whether constructions of upright or recumbent stones, or grassy mounds or embankments. Many sites crown lonely and elevated positions in the Peak, forming a conspicuous part of the scenery, and their occasionally ethereal atmosphere, together with numerous interpretations as to their purpose, has brought them into association with legends, superstition, long-surviving ancient customs and beliefs in earth mysteries. Whatever the reality behind the varied conjectures, the county's ancient sites belong both to its landscape and folklore heritage.

Strange magical tales indeed surround the Nine Ladies' Stone Circle on Stanton Moor and the Ninestones Circle on nearby Harthill Moor, names which in themselves emphasise a bygone significance attributed to the number nine. Its meaning is nowadays uncertain, yet this theme has recurred repeatedly not just in connection with similar sites throughout Britain but in ritual ceremonies and mythologies from northern Europe to south-east Aia, in which it reputedly symbolised death and re-birth. To people whose economy had undergone a profound change, this second notion, embodied in the regeneration of the land each spring, was paramount for their survival, for after hundreds of millennia of a food-gathering economy this still-sparse population became increasingly dependent on food production from the New Stone Age onwards. If, as is often believed, stone circles were sacred shrines linked with fertility rites regarding the annual cycle of growth, they were central to the pattern of death and re-birth. However, this symbolism could have referred in another sense to the departure of the dead from earthly existence and entry into the after-life, a belief which evidence from graves has shown was strongly held by some early farming communities.

A rather different earthly pattern, intriguingly apparent on Ordnance Survey maps, is the way ancient sites seem to 'line up' together along remarkably straight lines popularly known as ley lines. Both the Ninestones and Nine Ladies' Circles are directly aligned with Derbyshire's main henge monument at Arbor Low, the invisible straight lines passing through burial mounds on the way. Not for nothing is Arbor Low termed locally the 'Stonehenge of the North', for it ranks third in importance only behind the mighty Stonehenge and Avebury in Wiltshire. But claims of up to one hundred and fifty ley lines emanating from it have caused the monument to be described as a veritable New Stone Age and Bronze Age 'Spaghetti Junction', especially if, as once thought, the lines originally marked ancient trackways. Such assertions have invariably been dismissed – and yet a straight trackway possibly pre-dating Arbor Low ran close by across the White Peak plateau, linking it with other major haunts of the first farmers such as Minninglow and Harborough Rocks. The trackway's course is still discernible: it provided an obvious route for a later Roman road, in use for many centuries.

Minninglow

On its progression north towards another henge monument called the Bull Ring, at Dove Holes, the track passed near Thirst House Cave in Deepdale, one of several ancient places in Derbyshire named after Hob Hurst or 'Hob i' th' Hurst', a temperamental woodland spirit, who in local lore was reputed to inhabit remote forest and burial sites. His magical powers were said to bring harmony and discord alternately to the rural population as late as the 19th century, and aroused so much fear of harm in some countryfolk that his abodes inspired a sense of awe and mystery. Through this piece of folklore came a situation quite in reverse to that of the New Stone Age farmers who, instead of fearing forest spirits, had to cut down and burn trees in order to create clearings where they could grow their crops and allow their herds to graze.

The New Stone Age economy based on food production from crops and domesticated animals, but still employing stone and bone (as opposed to metal) implements, is generally termed Neolithic. Its development enabled settlement to become more permanent and, although hunting continued as a dietary supplement, a sufficient food surplus supported specialised craftworkers in the production of tools and pottery. Such changes appear to have influenced Derbyshire only some five hundred years after the first influx of Neolithic folk into Britain around 3500 B.C. and even then the old nomadic lifestyle survived until the new was eventually assimilated by the native hunting population. Mesolithic tools have been found close to Neolithic settlement sites, for example at Willington, where easily-worked soils above flood level made the Trent river-terraces particularly attractive to the farmers of this and several subsequent ages. Evidence from here and Aston-upon-Trent, the location of another settlement and a mysterious 5,700 feet long and 300 feet wide earthwork called a cursus, showed that the earliest crops cultivated in the area were barley and wheat. Domesticated animals included cattle, pigs, sheep and goats.

From White Peak caves and open areas have been identified many examples of the chief tools used in the onslaught against the forests: polished stone axes, for which flint remained in demand, but even more popular were the hard-wearing volcanic rocks of the Lake District. The

Neolithic leaf-shaped arrowhead from Rains Cave, and Bronze Age 'barbed and tanged' from Arbor Low

Lakeland 'axe factories' at Langdale became the most productive in Britain, and to ensure that the tools reached their various markets, a network of long-distance trade routes developed. Wherever possible, obvious landmarks such as ridges or upland plateaux were favoured for these routes. Such features, being so well-drained on the Carboniferous limestone terrain, at last boosted the White Peak in importance: the ancient ridgeway between Lose Hill and Mam Tor on the northern 'boundary' with the Dark Peak is still one of the county's most impressive hill-walks; south-west of this, the undulating top of the limestone plateau allowed for the very direct route past Arbor Low; more winding was a track known to later ages as the Portway which began in Nottinghamshire and traversed high ground on the eastern side of the Peak, one branch of it heading also for Mam Tor. The routes from here and Arbor Low then seem to have converged near the Bull Ring with another from the west.

The proximity of the henge monuments to the main Peakland thoroughfares lends support to the view that they were focal points for the seasonal gatherings of large numbers of people – though whether these were for religious observances, trade, celebrations similar to medieval fairs, or a combination of all three, is not clear. A henge basically consisted of a circular area, sometimes with a stone or timber circle, surrounded by a ditch and an outer embankment of earth, broken by between one and four entrances. Their origin has been dated to the late Neolithic period prior to 2000 B.C. but the significance of some, of which Low Arbor is a well-preserved example, far transcended their first phase of use. Arbor Low and the Bull Ring are each about two hundred and fifty feet in diameter, have two entrances and an accompanying circular mound less than four hundred yards to the south-west. But a curious extra detail visible at Arbor Low is the 'serpentine ridge of earth' between the henge and its mound, Gib Hill. Adjacent to the latter is also the site of an earlier monument which occupied more of a hill-top position than its successor and was closer to the trackway. Gib Hill itself covers a previous mound (a Bronze Age barrow), while Arbor Low 'Mark II' is guarded at its southern entrance by an additional circular mound post-dating the monument. Appropriately enough, its circle of recumbent stones has been noted as resembling a giant timepiece: whether or not they ever stood erect has been the subject of much debate, which remains unresolved. Excavations showed no proof of socket holes for holding upright stones. However, they certainly differ in composition from the limestone of the immediate vicinity and so were transported to the site, probably on sledges made up of two wooden runners bound together by cross-timbers.

Jet necklace from a burial mound near Arbor Low

The sheer scale of organisation and labour involved in constructing such a monument by a society dependent still on antler picks and bone shovels most likely indicates an increasing complexity in the social hierarchy towards the end of the Neolithic period. Britain's first tribal

1. Stone Age cave entrance near the top of Creswell Crags.

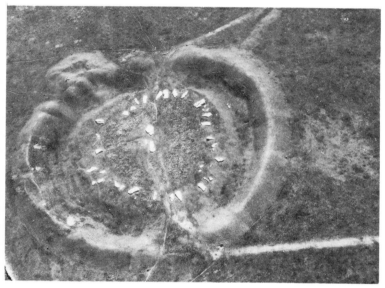

2. Arbor Low: aerial view.

3. Bronze Age burial cist, Gib Hill: composed of four vertical slabs and a capstone of Carboniferous limestone, its excavation by Thomas Bateman in 1848 revealed an urn containing cremated human bones.

4. Sheepwash Bridge, Ashford-in-the-Water, near which the ancient Portway route forded the Derbyshire Wye.

5. The Benty Grange helmet, now part of the Bateman Collection in Sheffield Museum. The iron framework, with silver-plated rivets and early Christian cross on the nosepiece, was originally over a protective head-covering of horn. The boar, a pagan Saxon symbol, is about 3½ inches long and consists of two D-shaped bronze pieces joined together along the spine and held by four silver rivets. Its body is studded with silver, the eyes and tusks with gold.

6. Peveril Castle, Castleton: the dominating symbol of Norman authority in the High Peak. Established soon after the Conquest, its 12th-century keep is about sixty feet high, with walls eight feet thick. The earthwork in the foreground is part of Castleton's medieval town boundary and the flags on the hillside were so placed for the 900th anniversary celebration of Domesday in 1986.

7. Chesterfield's oldest inn, the *Royal Oak*, was originally a rest house for the order of military monks, the Knights Templar, during the Crusades. Situated in The Shambles, where other buildings from medieval times survived until the late 19th century, the inn was restored in 1900.

8. Fenny Bentley Hall, the moated and fortified medieval manor of the Beresford family, today a farmhouse, retains some of its original structure.

9. The brass memorial to Sir Nicholas and Lady Joanna Kniveton, dated 1475, in Muggington church, is one of the most attractive in the county. Sir Nicholas, lord of the manors of Mercaston and Underwood, wears the traditional Lancastrian 'SS' collar. Attached to this is a small portcullis, originally the badge of the Beaufort family, descendants of John of Gaunt: through Margaret Beaufort, Countess of Derby and mother of King Henry VII, this eventually became the badge of the Tudor dynasty. The fox on Sir Nicholas's helmet appears to have been a personal crest.

10. (*above*) Norman doorway, Steetley Chapel. Measuring just 52 feet long by 15 feet wide, tradition tells that Robin Hood's follower, Alan a Dale, was married here. The chapel was restored in 1882.

11. (*above right*) Chesterfield's famous church with the crooked spire belonged to the Dean and Chapter of Lincoln Cathedral from 1100-1884. The present cruciform building, its tower and 228-feet spire, date mostly from the 14th century. Lead plates laid in a herring-bone pattern accentuate the twist on the spire, which may have been caused by the heavy weight of the lead after its timber substructure had warped.

12. (*right*) 'The Cathedral of the Peak', Tideswell: a 14th-century church which reflects the prosperity of the medieval wool trade. The Foljambe family were major benefactors.

chieftains are usually assumed to have been men powerful enough to organise the required workforce (though some may have been women – the later, more martial Iron Age was not averse to female leaders!). Status symbols such as ornamented pottery and weapons, and rare pieces of personal jewellery found in many ancient Peakland graves clearly testify to the establishment of an aristocratic elite by the time of the Bronze Age. Burial sites of Neolithic and Bronze Age date occur in abundance around Arbor Low, rather like Christian tombs around a church or cathedral, and almost every summit has its own 'low' visible against the skyline – in Derbyshire, this word is most often equated with its Old English meaning of a mound, and appears more frequently than the alternative terms of 'tumulus' or 'round barrow'. The age-old affinity between tombs and places of worship indeed suggests that Arbor Low was a sanctuary but, during the thousand years or so of its active use, the funereal practices of the local inhabitants underwent many changes.

Bronze Age food vessel, Arbor Low, and collared urn, Flax Dale

Stone cists or chambers capped with horizontal slabs contained the dead beneath the mounds. Neolithic chambered tombs were usually connected with the outside by approach passages and were the centres of multiple interments, though these probably took place in several stages. The burial rite was inhumation, but there is evidence that bodies were exposed to weathering beforehand. Minninglow, with four known burial chambers, was the largest of these tombs in Derbyshire; at Ringham Low, the skulls and bones of 18 people were discovered; the skeletons from the two back-to-back chambers at Five Wells tomb numbered 17 and, at Stoney Low, a total of 161 teeth were amongst the contents of one grave! In physical appearance, the Neolithic farmers were small in height and 'long-headed'. The latter part of the period saw the arrival of people with a more 'round-headed' appearance who preferred to bury their dead in caves, skulls separated from the skeletons and sometimes a dog interred with its master. A rock shelter in Calling Low Dale housed grave goods including decorated Neolithic pottery known as Peterborough Ware, intended presumably to accompany its dead into the next world, and also a burial, foetus fashion, in a crouched position: when the first metalworkers arrived in Derbyshire, this form of interment, together with richer grave goods, became prevalent.

The proliferation of burial mounds coincided with a climate milder than today's. During the Bronze Age, two – or possibly three – waves of immigration influenced both highland and lowland, extending cereal-growing temporarily to the gritstone moorlands. Yet ironically, the different groups of metalworkers have been distinguished by three types of pottery they entombed with their dead: Beaker folk, Food Vessel folk and Urnfolk. They also left behind ridged bands of gold, bronze axes and daggers from Ireland, necklaces of jet from North Yorkshire and glass faience beads, the star-shaped and segmented examples unearthed at Doll Tor on Stanton Moor being one of possibly only five known in Britain, similar to one from a chambered tomb on the Isles of Scilly.

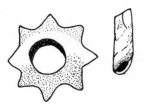

Bronze Age faience beads, Doll Tor, Stanton Moor

Gib Hill tumulus and ridged earthwork snaking from Arbor Low

Around 2000 B.C. the round-headed Beaker folk entered the White Peak and Trent valley from the south and east. Their metal implements were at first produced from copper, but with improving knowledge, from the alloy of copper and tin which gives its name to the era they ushered in. Despite their innovations, however, evidence – again from Peakland sites – seems to show that the native Neolithic way of life continued. For besides the customary high-necked beakers integral to the newcomers' burial rites, grave goods frequently included barbed and tanged flint arrowheads, yet the contrasting Neolithic leaf-shaped versions found, for example in the Harborough chambered tomb, also more surprisingly featured in a Bronze Age mound on Stanton Moor. Both types occurred at Arbor Low, which may mean simultaneous use. The circle's central arrangement of stones – or 'cove' – may have symbolised to each culture an entrance to the next world.

As revealed by the finds from Gib Hill and the nowadays pock-marked barrow adjoining Arbor Low, Bronze Age burials tended to be individual rather than communal. The original mound at Gib Hill was seemingly not for 'sepulchral' purposes – the only burial cist lay unusually near the top of the superimposed tumulus. The interments here and in the other barrow reflected a later Bronze Age development in that they were cremations, but one of the attendant food vessels represented a mixture of the flat-bottomed tradition of Beaker pottery with the wide-necked style of Neolithic, a form first apparent in Derbyshire in the Trent valley before 1600 B.C. But whether its introduction was the result of more incomers into this area or an adaptation by already settled Neolithic and Beaker descendants is not known.

This culture endured for maybe less than a century before a different wide-necked vessel called the collared urn made its appearance in the Peak with new settlers from the north-west. The Urnfolk used such pottery to store cremated bones and soon the Food Vessel folk took up the practice with their own. The environmental conditions then allowed for arable farming on the lower-lying gritstone areas, but their lack of cultivation since the Bronze Age has fortunately helped to preserve the Urnfolk's settlement sites as well as ritual and burial: for instance, at Gardom's Edge near Baslow where remains exist of huts, fields, an enclosure – probably for protecting herds overnight from wolves – and several engraved rock patterns known as 'cup-and-ring markings'. These consist of small cup-shaped depressions in the rock encircled by incised rings and constitute another ancient feature whose meaning is a mystery. If they were magical/religious symbols, the location of further examples on Rowter Rocks near Stanton Moor is especially apt, for although Bronze Age stone circles and tumuli are numerous on the gritstone moors, nowhere is the concentration as great as in the square-mile area of Stanton Moor which has over seventy burial mounds.

The central legend concerning the small, upright stones of the Nine Ladies' Circle on this moor – that the 'ladies' were turned to stone for

Patterned beaker, Grindlow near Tideswell

dancing on the sabbath to the music of a fiddler, who became the circle's outlying King Stone – does at least accord with the idea that this was a holy place. The circle once had a burial cist in its midst, and though the function allotted to the King Stone remains unclear, like Gib Hill it stands on higher ground south-west of its stone circle. Bronze Age cemeteries such as Stanton Moor were for individuals important enough to own bronze weapons, expensive items compared with their stone counterparts until about 1100 B.C. After this, the addition of locally-mined lead to the other metals eventually made bronze more easily obtainable.

Ridgeway route, Mam Tor

A society able to produce a consistent agricultural surplus and later supply an important raw material had the wealth to accumulate rich commodities, but as so often throughout the ages that wealth belonged to a powerful few. Perhaps from the desire to acquire more by dominating the trade routes which the Peak's central position controlled, tribal warfare began. Across Harthill Moor a former stretch of the Portway is now the main footpath passing by defended Bronze Age homestead sites near Robin Hood's Stride and Cratcliffe Tor, the Ninestones Circle (linked in local legends with fairy music and dancing when there is a full moon!) and, shortly, the strategically-placed earthwork of Castle Ring, a later-constructed hill-fort.

Derbyshire's hills offered many favourable sites for the construction of forts and, as Map 3 shows, most were built on positions to command lines of communication. They are generally dated to the Iron Age, but excavations at Mam Tor hill-fort indicated occupation there from the late Bronze Age. With its extensive views across the Dark and White Peak, by then mostly denuded of forest cover, this was the largest and highest hill-fort and had the added advantage of a perennial water supply from the spring at its north-west corner – unlike the fort at Fin Cop, perched on precipitous limestone slopes above Monsal Dale. Such was the latter's natural defensive position, however, that man-made fortifications were only necessary on the eastern side, overlooking the Portway.

Ramparts with ditches outside each embankment were a security aspect of forts contrasting totally with the inward ditch-and-bank arrangements at henge monuments. In times of danger, Fin Cop no doubt afforded temporary refuge to local farming groups and their animals. It may also have been a corral for grazing stock overnight. Mam Tor, despite its proven use in the Bronze Age, has a name derived from Iron Age Celtic for 'rock' or 'mother rock'. Within the 16 acres enclosed – apart from on its famous crumbling shale cliff – by a rampart and ditch, was a permanent protected village of about a hundred circular huts, foundations of which are still perceptible as small hollows. The adoption of strong but inexpensive iron tools and weapons made both farming and fighting more efficient, and as the ages termed 'prehistoric' neared their close, for the first time written records contemporary to the

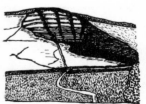

Mam Tor

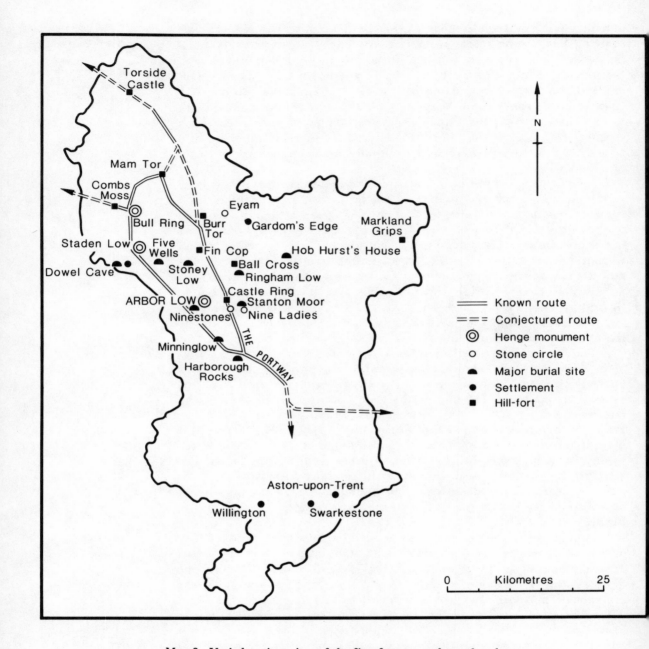

Map 3. Varied ancient sites of the first farmers and metalworkers.

Torside
Castle

Mam Tor

Combs
Moss

Eyam

Gardom's Edge

Markland
Grips

Bull Ring
Burr
Tor

Staden Low
Five
Wells

Fin Cop

Hob Hurst's House

Dowel Cave

Stoney
Low

Ball Cross

Ringham Low

ARBOR LOW

Castle Ring

Stanton Moor

Ninestones

Nine Ladies

THE PORTWAY

Minninglow

Harborough
Rocks

Known route
Conjectured route
Henge monument
Stone circle
Major burial site
Settlement
Hill-fort

Aston-upon-Trent

Willington

Swarkestone

0   Kilometres   25

N

period began to add to future knowledge. The picture these suggested of a north-south divide in Iron Age Derbyshire life is corroborated by archaeological evidence.

The arrival of the iron-using people called Celts occurred in Britain around 500 B.C. and in the following centuries the southern half of the country became well-populated. In Derbyshire there was, as before, some overlap between the old and new cultures, but the spreading use of iron meant that White Peak lead was no longer required by the southern tribes. Iron was much cheaper to produce than bronze, because its ore was extensively available and smelting could be undertaken by self-sufficient local communities, using charcoal provided by tree clearance. South Derbyshire reflected the general prosperity of its southern neighbours within a rigidly-structured society, and settlement along the Trent river-terraces continued apace. Sites at Willington again revealed the pattern of mixed farming from previous ages, but a typical farmstead was now organised into a large, circular, main farmhouse and amid the openness of the surrounding fields many smaller round huts which probably housed farm labourers or even slaves. The domestic work involved textile-weaving, the making of coarse pottery (apparently no longer for funerary use) and much cereal grinding.

Roman writers relate that this area lay within the province of a Midland tribe called the Coritani, but the less peaceful area to the north seems to have formed a 'border country' between them and a great northern tribe called the Brigantes. The possibility of skirmishes and frequent cattle-raids in a region already impoverished by the ceasing demand for lead, combined with a colder climate which had meant the gritstone moorland settlements being long since abandoned, paints a literally bleak view of north Derbyshire. Compared with the beautiful Bronze Age jewellery found in the Peak, Iron Age finds have been very poor, the finest piece being a brooch from Harborough Cave.

But to this then unstable land, with its stone circles and mounds, the Celts brought traditions which have lingered in the county perhaps as in no other. Their religion was based on beliefs in spirits, some of whom dwelt in burial mounds, or else woods, springs or streams. Maybe Hob Hurst originated from Celtic lore. In the province of Brigantia, all deities were subject to the mother goddess of the same name – the life-giving goddess of water. North Derbyshire's well-dressings and Castleton's Garland Ceremony, to which fuller reference will be made in later chapters, could emanate from the worship of her; the custom of 'church clipping' is linked to the Celtic worship of stones and the once-popular practice of carrying maidens' garlands at the funerals of young, unmarried girls was also of Celtic origin – although, like well-dressing, its beginnings have often been credited to the Romans. In fact, these conquerors of Celtic rule in Britain, so powerful and dominant in the lowland south and east, were to find the 'Romanisation' of Iron-Age Derbyshire, particularly amongst its hills, much more of a two-way process.

III   Under Roman Rule

By the time Roman soldiers marched past Arbor Low and Minninglow along their road called 'The Street', Derbyshire's Neolithic monuments were already 2,000 years old. This road, which followed the north-west/south-east direction of the ancient trade route across the limestone plateau, linked the Roman town of Aquae Arnemetiae (Buxton) with Derventio, the second of their forts at Derby, both names from Celtic influences – the town from the dedication of its warm spring-waters to the local goddess Arnemetia, the fort from the river Derwent which flowed nearby. This county of highland and lowland was valuable to the Roman economy for the production of 'Derbyshire Ware', orange to grey earthenware pottery, described by John Gillam as 'like petrified goose flesh', which has been found as far north as Scotland's Antonine Wall and even in disturbed burial chambers at Minninglow; but the major industry was the mining of lead – one of 'the rewards of victory', according to the Roman historian Tacitus. Yet that victory, hard-won against the inhabitants of the Peak, was no easy matter to consolidate.

The might of Ancient Rome has nevertheless been duly respected in local traditions. Near Whaley Bridge, a U-shaped hill-top valley called the Roosdyche was once reputed to have been a Roman construction for sports such as chariot-racing, but is now regarded as a legacy of the Ice Age. The Blue John Caverns near Castleton, formed by meltwater from the last glaciation, have their 'Roman level', indicating that Derbyshire's semi-precious Blue John stone was known to the Romans, a discovery no doubt made in their 'hunger' for lead. However, claims that they worked this stone and that Blue John vases were found in the ruins of Pompeii have been confounded by the knowledge that their source was another fluorspar from northern Italy. This mountainous area may also shed further light on the origin of well-dressing, for an ancient flower festival in its Alpine region in the 19th century recalled fond memories of the Derbyshire custom for the author William Howitt. The Romans, like the Celts, believed in spirits of woods and streams, and there is the possibility that both practised placating their water-spirits by decking springs with flowers. In Derbyshire, the Roman naming of Buxton and inscriptive evidence such as a gritstone altar dedicated to the god Mars linked with a Celtic deity Braciaca denote the conquerors' adoption of native cults into their religion – these may have included well-dressing, which later blended into Christian settings. The Romans certainly

Roman gritstone altar, Haddon Hall: 'To the god Mars Braciaca, Quintus Sittius Caecilianus, Prefect of the 1st Cohort of the Aquitani, performs his vow'

considered the water-goddess Brigantia to be the equal of their own chief god, Jupiter.

Roman milestone, Buxton, indicating the distance to Navio (Brough)

The expansion of the Roman Empire to include Britain was accomplished gradually in the years following A.D. 43. Within five years, the new province extended to a frontier along the Trent and the Romans faced a choice between invading the Brigantian hill country to the north or anti-Roman Wales. The Brigantes' Queen, Cartimandua, was pro-Roman and succeeded in maintaining her people's independence for over twenty years, although unrest inside her realm, caused partly because she abandoned her consort in favour of another man, made her require occasional Roman military aid, particularly when she handed the fugitive guerrilla leader, Caractacus, over to his imperial enemies in A.D. 51. They had by then crossed the Trent and established forts on Brigantia's very edge, the chain including Chesterfield and Strutt's Park, Derby. Civil War between pro- and anti-Roman factions within the northern tribe finally caused permanent annexation of their lands in A.D. 69-70, but the Peak District was not garrisoned until the governorship of Agricola in A.D.78-85.

The two key forts were built at Little Chester, Derby (Derventio) and Brough (Navio), which gained its name as well as a natural defensive position from the river Noe, being sited near the confluence with the Bradwell Brook. Others appeared at Buxton and Melandra near Glossop (Ardotalia), plus a fortlet at Pentrich midway between Little Chester and Chesterfield. These square-shaped Roman strongholds, with their distinctive rounded corners, bore scant resemblance to Iron Age forts. Protected first by turf and timber but later by stone-wall defences, their standardised internal layout included armouries, store-houses, the commander's house and rather less luxurious accommodation for 500 soldiers. Outside each fort, a civilian settlement called a *vicus* developed, containing shops, inns, temples and brothels amongst the varied buildings. Melandra's *vicus* is known to have been built about the same time as the Agricolan fort, and at Buxton the great attraction of the thermal springs soon transformed the *vicus* into a spa-town ranking in status only behind Bath. Its lead-lined Roman baths were still in use in Tudor times, during which a Roman statue, possibly inscribed Arne for Arnemetia, was 'miraculously' discovered and believed then to be an image of St Anne, the well's Christian patroness.

Linking Brough with Buxton was 'the road to the bath', known later as Batham Gate. Its course is still partly in use, as also is that of 'The Street'. Both roads traversed fairly easy terrain and required minimal constructional work, unlike routes over the Dark Peak such as Doctor's Gate between Brough and Melandra, of which a paved section still exists on Coldharbour Moor. Roman finds, especially of pottery, near the pre-existing Portway attest to its continued use, its eastern branch possibly sharing a part route with Doctor's Gate. Melandra lies some three miles south-west of Torside Castle detailed on Map 3 and a

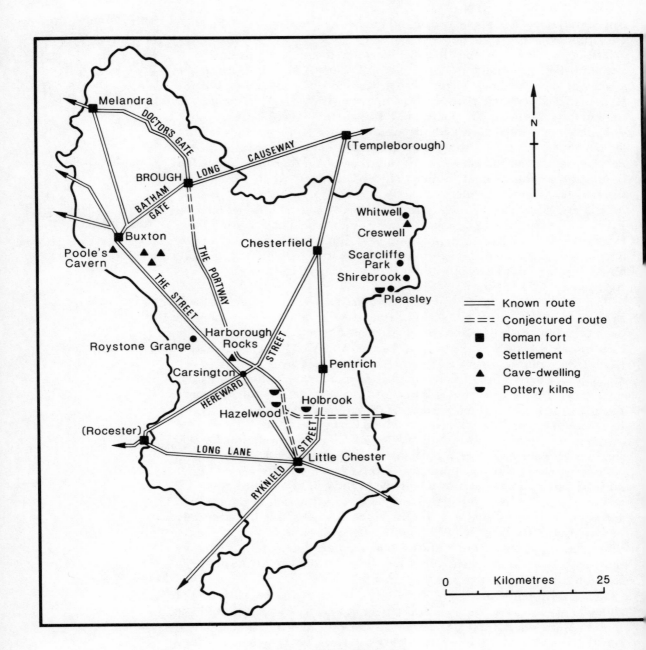

Map 4. Roman Derbyshire.

trackway joining the latter with this Roman road is nowadays a stretch of the rugged Pennine Way. Known and conjectured routes on Map 4, connecting forts less than a day's march apart, show a system designed to contain potential hostility amongst the native population. The Romans' assumption that they had subjugated the Peak enough to allow abandonment of their forts around A.D. 140, in order to provide troops for invading Scotland, was proved wrong by subsequent native revolts. Ludworth Moor near Melandra is said to be the site of a battle between Romans and Britons. An inscription found at Brough recorded its rebuilding and occupation by the 1st cohort (infantry) of the Aquitanians when Julius Verus was Britain's Governor – around A.D.115-8. Little Chester was also reoccupied, and again there were local risings around A.D. 165. Brough was not finally abandoned until A.D. 350-60. Its long existence resulted from the need for military control over the adjacent lead-mining areas, for which it served too as a commercial centre. Beneath the administrative headquarters was a closely-guarded underground strongroom where the soldiers' pay was kept.

A census officer was responsible for surveillance over the natives who dwelt in the fort's *vicus*, but the actual mining often involved using convict labour or slaves. A tradition grew up in Brough that the nearby village of Bradwell had been a Roman penal colony for convicts sentenced to work in the lead-mines. Wirksworth has a similar tradition regarding its Middleton neighbour. Multi-purpose lead was required by the Romans for water-pipes, cisterns, roofs, bath buildings, caskets and coffins. Mining was mostly opencast – at the Roman farmstead of Roystone Grange near Minninglow, evidence of on-site smelting was also found. Farther south along The Street, where its line intersected Hereward Street, the civilian settlement of Carsington has been postulated as the yet unidentified lead-mining centre of Lutudarum inscribed LVT on many ingots, or pigs, of Derbyshire lead. The discoveries of these mainly in the south-east of the limestone plateau has long given support to claims that this place was in the Wirksworth-Matlock area, yet curiously an ingot recovered from Owslow Farm near Carsington bore no such inscription. Inscribed lead ingots from Derbyshire have been found in Nottinghamshire and South Yorkshire. There were probably trade routes *via* the river Don to the Humber and the major site of Petuaria; at least one ingot has been found in Gaul.

The manufacture of Derbyshire Ware was also concentrated southeast of the White Peak, between Wirksworth and Derby. The main production centres were sited at Holbrook and Hazelwood, close to the Portway, but the earliest kilns, probably military in origin, were in operation at Little Chester before A.D. 120. Although mass production began as a localised industry, an expanding market for the pottery came especially from the northern garrisons, continuing into the fourth century. Other kiln sites were at Shottle and also in the Magnesian limestone area at Pleasley. Finds of Derbyshire Ware on native sites within the county, whether farmsteads or caves, have been extensive.

Pigs of Derbyshire lead 'from the mines of Lutudarum'

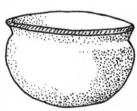

Derbyshire Ware, Rains Cave, and Roman urn found containing a coin hoard, Shipley

33

An unusual aspect of life in Roman Derbyshire was the native propensity still to inhabit caves. Creswell Crags again provided shelter during this period in which the Magnesian limestone ridge was generally populous, evidence of settlements being known at Scarcliffe Park near Langwith, Whitwell and Shirebrook, in addition to Pleasley. Some Carboniferous limestone caves became permanent living-quarters close to Buxton and The Street. At the much-occupied Harborough Cave, problems of waterlogging in wet weather were solved by laying a thick floor of rubble which allowed better drainage. Probably also an overhead framework of poles covered with skins diverted water dripping from the roof to drain off at the sides. Excavations uncovered spears and iron tools of the second and third centuries, horse-riding equipment, Roman coins, spindle-whorls, a bone weaving comb and jewellery including a rare intaglio of Rome's goddess of wisdom, Minerva. However, the general picture from native sites is of a self-sufficient way of life hardly changed since the Iron Age, and to which Roman rule had brought little marked improvement. (North Derbyshire seems never to have become fully Romanised like Lincolnshire, South Yorkshire and the eastern side of Nottinghamshire.) New crops such as rye were introduced, but partly to help feed the imperial army. The Romans' stimulus of the economy largely to their own ends did not outlast their departure. Even before then, the farmstead at Roystone Grange, which had an aisled farmhouse (an early form of villa) in the second century and may have been worked by colonial descendants, apparently failed to maintain its prosperity.

In A.D. 313 Christianity was officially recognised by the Roman Empire. A Bishop of Lincoln was in office by the following year, but there is little evidence of Christian penetration into Derbyshire. Perhaps one of its effects was to discourage the occasional 'pagan' tendency to inter Roman corpses in Bronze Age barrows. Unlike the bygone funerary urns, however, fourth-century Roman urns were more likely to be used by their owners for the secret burial of coin hoards, a symptom maybe of the growing insecurity then as 'barbarian' raids by Angles, Saxons, Picts and Scots undermined Roman Britain's stability. Gradually, troops were withdrawn to stem similar attacks at the Empire's heart and, with the collapse of centralised authority so long enforced by the Roman army, the political organisation of Derbyshire disintegrated back into local tribes, faced with new invaders.

IV Saxon Derbyshire

Dark and forbidding, the undated hill-fort of Carl Wark on the moors east of Hathersage was once thought to be pre-Roman, but more usually nowadays as post-Roman, a silent monument to troubled times. If so, this fort, with its massive gritstone defences, is a somewhat graphic reminder that the centuries following the fall of Rome are called the Dark Ages. Across the Roman Batham Gate in Bradwell Dale, a longitudinal earthwork possessing the slightly less sombre name of Grey Ditch may, around the early seventh century, have been a territorial and defensive boundary thrown up by Saxons in an attempt to limit access into the White Peak for the unconquered Britons to the north.

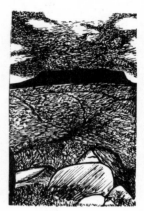

Carl Wark

There is certainly no trace of concerted Anglo-Saxon progress into the Peak before this date, which infers that the Celtic descendants peopling Derbyshire's hill country preserved their independence and a measure of insularity for over two hundred years after the Romans departed, continuing the traditional farming life – and probably also lead-mining, plus perpetuating their forebears' worship of 'fountains and stones' still widespread even amongst some early Christians. One idea put forward is that a British kingdom prevailed here during this time, with a fortified capital on Win Hill overlooking the Hope valley. Defensive ditches exist on its slopes, but legend tells that a victorious seventh-century army was encamped on this hill and their adversaries on nearby Lose Hill before a great battle raged, the outcome of which determined their corresponding names. The victors were led by a converted Christian – Edwin, King of Saxon Northumbria, against a joint force from the Saxon realms of Wessex and Mercia under the latter's pagan king, Penda. Roman roads and towns had generally fallen into disuse throughout Britain long before, but it is possible that Penda's army entered the Peak via The Street from the Mercian village of Northworthy which had developed near the *vicus* settlement outside the abandoned fort of Little Chester.

One of the earliest and finest signs of Anglo-Saxon presence in the White Peak was, however, more reminiscent of the Bronze Age in being the burial mound of a warrior lord accompanied by rich grave goods. Benty Grange lies close to The Street between Arbor Low and Buxton, and the contents of its tumulus displayed a mixture of both Christian and pagan symbolism. Silver crosses adorned a leather drinking cup and the nosepiece of a helmet which has become famous far beyond

Leather drinking cup, Benty Grange

35

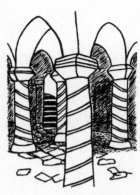

Saxon crypt, Repton

Derbyshire, for its remains were surmounted by a bronze boar decorated with gold and silver, a distinctive crest alluded to in the epic Anglo-Saxon poem *Beowulf* of a century later. Roman writers had also made reference to the boar crest on the helmets of 'Germanic' tribes and its sacred affiliation with their god, Freyr, whose protection was being sought in battle.

Penda ultimately triumphed with Edwin's defeat and death in South Yorkshire in A.D. 634 and the consequent aftermath of Mercian ascendancy probably contributed to the movement of Saxon settlers at last into the region they called 'Peaclond'. (The first written references to the area came in Anglo-Saxon chronicles of the seventh and tenth centuries.) The kingdom of Mercia had been established with Penda's grandfather Crida as its first king before A.D. 590 and comprised most of the Midlands, southern Derbyshire being quickly valued as an important nucleus. For as in previous ages, the county's highland and lowland histories were different. Angle and Saxon invaders had first penetrated inland along navigable rivers and so had settled on the Trent river-terraces within half a century of the Roman withdrawal from Britain. But their introduction of heavy ox-drawn ploughs allowed them also to cultivate the more difficult soils of valley floors and clay soils of the lowlands between Peak and the Trent. The number of settlements near the Derwent with names ending in -ley (for example Beeley, Darley, Rowsley), from the Anglo-Saxon for 'a woodland pasturage', suggests that its valley bottom was still thickly wooded. Other county place-names of Anglo-Saxon origin have endings of -ford,-wich, -worth, -bury, -well and most commonly -ton, meaning an enclosure, or -ington (sometimes -inton), a hybrid of -ton and -ing, which denoted possession. Thus the village of Mugginton, for instance, may be derived from the farmstead of a Saxon lord with the grand name of Mugga!

From -ton the word 'town' originates, but the ending itself is sometimes directly equated with village or manor as alternatives to enclosure – and with good reason, for the Anglo-Saxons added centralised rural villages to the settlement pattern of individual farmsteads. Often several villages were subsidiary to a main village where the local noble family who controlled the district dwelt in greater splendour than the rest of the population in their small, rectangular huts. The villages especially in south and east Derbyshire were surrounded by large open fields, a characteristic of the Midlands for several centuries. However, the far-reaching implications of this hierarchical but more communal agricultural system were that in time all villages and their adjacent lands were organised into manors, each under the power and jurisdiction of its owner – whether lord or lady – and this system in turn did much to fashion the county's present-day countryside, with its different styles of villages and renowned manor houses.

The foremost settlement in Saxon Derbyshire was Repton, situated on a range of low hills just south of the Trent. Over the centuries its name has been more than variously spelt, but the earlier records always applied the ending -dun which apparently was taken from the Celtic for hill. Again local tradition adds to the story, imparting that Mercian kings were proclaimed and shown to the people on a hill here. True or not, the intimation of Repton's strong royal connections within the central Saxon kingdom is well-founded. The claim has been made that it was the capital of Mercia, which is probably correct concerning its role both as a political and religious centre, the setting first of a royal court and later the burial place of kings. Its importance grew as Mercia's power rose under Penda. He was killed in battle when aged over eighty in 655, a resolute pagan to the end. Nevertheless he had during his lifetime delegated the rule of his realm south of the Trent to his son and successor, Peada, whose marriage into the Northumbrian royal family, despite the bitter enmity between the two kingdoms, had brought Christianity to Mercia in 653 – and firstly, to Repton.

With the northern princess came four missionary priests, mentioned by the Venerable Bede as Cedd, Adda, Betti and Diuma, who was appointed the first Bishop of Mercia. In Derbyshire their work augmented further the Celtic influence, for the conversion of Mercia was the last major task confronting the Celtic Christian Church prior to its take-over by the Roman Church (a survivor of the imperial collapse) from 664 onwards. Before then, the two institutions had differed in the outward practice of their faith, disagreeing not least over when Easter should be held. An abbey had also been established at Repton 'under the old Saxon way', open to men and women equally but ruled by an abbess. Attached was a mausoleum where Mercian royalty were buried and later a shrine was built holding in reverence the murdered remains of a saintly prince called Wystan. This historic place now forms the well-known crypt beneath the chancel of Repton church. The 1979-excavated 'Repton Stone' displaying a mounted warrior with sword and shield may have been part of an eighth-century king's tombstone.

The leadership of an abbess over a mixed community highlights the better status of women at this time compared with subsequent ages. The Anglo-Saxons accorded with the Celts in accepting women in authority over men, whether in government, military leadership or high religious office. Christianity began to erode female equality but the 'Saxon way' more than upheld it.

Around Wirksworth, the Mercian rulers had, like their Roman predecessors, appropriated the lead-mines for their own enrichment, but the rights over these mines were granted to the abbesses of Repton and held by them for almost two centuries. In 714 the Abbess Eadburgha sent from Wirksworth to Crowland, Lincolnshire, a lead coffin for the burial of St Guthlac, who had begun his monastic life at Repton during the 690s after a rather unruly youth in the Mercian army. A Saxon memorial of about this date found in Wirksworth church, however, was not of lead but a remarkable stone carved with gospel scenes, including Christ

Ancient lead miner, Wirksworth church

*Anglo-Saxon jewellery
from the Peak*

washing his disciples' feet, the Crucifixion, Resurrection and Ascension. The skeleton beneath it was believed to be that of Betti, this church's traditional founder, whose missionary work was probably centred here. Another stone fittingly portrays an ancient lead miner carrying his pick and kibble.

Wirksworth's mines reappeared in Christmas records in 835 when the Abbess Kenewara leased them to Duke Humbert, a Mercian nobleman, provided that he gave 300 shillings' worth of lead for the repair of Christ church, Canterbury. Other Dark Ages links are that the industry's chief official, the Barmaster, and the Barmote Courts which to this day oversee Peakland lead-mining matters are names maybe of Saxon derivation. Near Castleton, the Odin Mine is reputed by reason of its name after a pagan god of Norse mythology (Anglo-Saxon equivalent Woden) to be one of the locality's oldest mines.

An intermingling of old and new religions long pervaded Derbyshire's early Christian period, a fact made evident by finds such as those from Benty Grange. The placing of objects alongside the dead – and in burial mounds too – was doubly a pagan practice denounced by the Church, but in this time of transition Christian items were included, the most beautiful being perhaps the cross of gold set with a garnet, found at

Engraving of the late seventh-century Wirksworth Stone from Bygone Derbyshire *(1892). It is though to be the sepulchral stone of Betti, one of the four Northumbrian missionaries who brought Christianity to the central Saxon kingdom of Mercia. Its antiquity is such that the inclusion of a lamb on the cross near the top left corner predates a Church edict of A.D. 692 commanding that in future a human figure should represent images of Christ.*

38

Winster Moor. Many interments took place in Bronze Age mounds, so the quantity of Saxon barrows in the White Peak is small, but the quality of their contents reveals a society well able to support great craftsmanship. Jewellery of gold, silver and bronze set with a variety of precious stones often displays also a mixture of Saxon and Celtic influences, for example in the 'scroll' pattern favoured by craftsmen of both cultures. This seems to indicate a gradual mergence between invaders and natives, as had happened in the past when the newcomers stayed permanently. Elsewhere in Derbyshire, the story of a living population adapting to different religious views is also partly told through the changing burial rituals regarding its dead. An early cemetery at Foremark near Repton consisted of burial mounds, but other Trent valley sites reverted to the Bronze Age custom of interring cremated bones in urns, though these were placed in the earth in trenches rather than mounds – as at King's Newton. After about A.D. 700 all pagan burial traditions ceased.

Progress towards the full adoption of Christianity then continued in harmony with a time of mainly peace and prosperity which lasted until about 850. Monastic annals recorded that in 757 King Ethelbald was buried 'at Repton'. Under his successor, Offa, Mercia became the most powerful realm in England. The blend of pagan and Christian symbolism together with Saxon and Celtic artwork was by then being seen on the more overtly Christian decorated stone crosses, which were erected amongst existing communities as the first focal points for Sunday sermons. Of Derbyshire's surviving examples, the most complete is at Eyam which depicts the Virgin and Child, and a profusion of angels, as well as interlacing knotwork and spiralling foliage. This last design is similar to that on Bakewell's cross, where it is said to represent Yggdrasil, the great ash tree of Norse legend, and the roughly-carved animal above it appearing to hold a nut in his forepaws – the squirrel Ratakosk, the symbol of life. In contrast, the other side of the cross displays the Crucifixion.

Also visible at Bakewell, inside the church porch, the collection of broken fragments of other crosses and numerous ancient gravestones dating from about A.D. 800 onwards implies a Saxon church of some importance being established on this site, connected with a small monastery. Diverse symbols, of probable Norman date, on the stones indicate the occupations of the deceased, including a chalice (priest), sword (soldier) and axe (woodman). At Blackwell in the Erewash valley and Spondon in the lower Derwent, the existence of a Saxon cross each near churches dedicated to Mercia's first saint, Werburgh (Penda's granddaughter), points to their early origin as places of Christian worship. Another St Werburgh's church was founded in Derbyshire's future county town, allegedly while it was still Anglo-Saxon Northworthy. Better documented, however, were two churches to St Chad, at Sawley and Wilne near the Trent-Derwent confluence, mentioned by 822. As

Saxon cross, Eyam

39

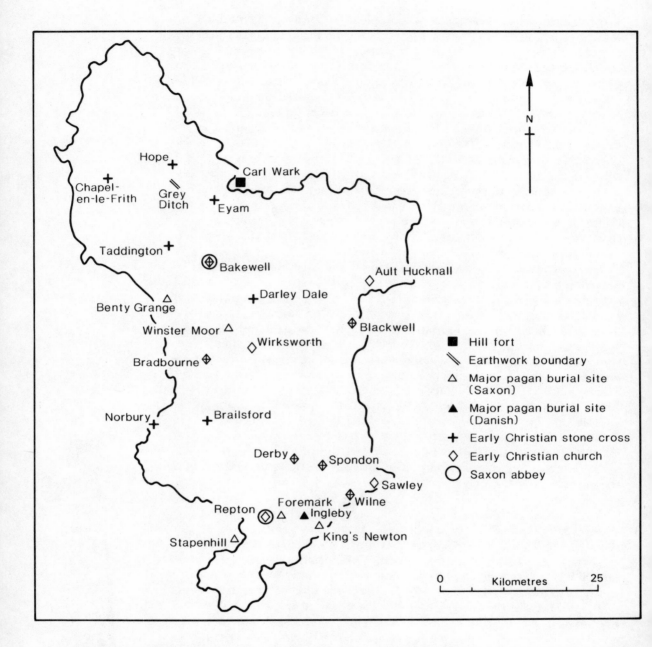

Map 5. Dark Age 'seeing the light': a gradual transition from pagan to some beginnings of Christian influence.

Christianity spread amongst the various settlements, parish boundaries were set up, often defined by the courses of ancient roads and trackways. Because the Peakland villages were more scattered, parishes there tended to cover extensive areas between 'streets' and 'ways', terms also of Saxon origin.

After King Offa's death in 796, Mercian dominance over the other Saxon kingdoms was gradually weakened by the rising power of Wessex, whose kings became rulers of all England from the 820s. But portents of change had already appeared as Vikings and Danes invaded from the east, directing their hostility especially towards the symbols of Christianity and eventually moving inland. By the winter of 874 they had reached Repton, from where they drove the Mercian King Burhed 'over sea' to refuge in Rome, laid waste the abbey and pillaged the surrounding area. Derbyshire's Saxon inhabitants were now faced with a threat similar to that posed by their own ancestors during and after the Roman withdrawal: invasion by fierce enemies 'with blue eyes and flowing hair, pagans in religion, worshipping the powers of nature'. The great difference was that in the heyday of Mercia the Saxons had added to the county's already ancient heritage a legacy on which future generations were literally to build.

Gold and garnet necklace, Galley Low near Brassington

V Danelaw

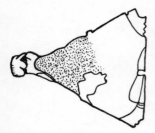

Viking axe-head, Repton

A ninth-century Viking axe-head, apparently separated from its handle by the impact of a forceful blow, was discovered over one thousand years later outside the chancel of Repton church. Rusted, but still awesome, it may provide physical evidence of the violent Scandinavian attack on the Mercian monastery there. That the army which wrought such destruction was largely Danish is borne out by contemporary records yet, even before this, an Anglo-Saxon chronicle in 871 had hinted at a constructive aspect of their local influence, referring to 'a place called Northworthy but Deoraby in the language of the Danes'. As Northworthy, the Mercian settlement commanding the Derwent valley had merely been north of a more important place, i.e. Repton; as Deoraby, the sole recorded instance of a place-name changed by Danes and soon consistently shortened to Derby, it quickly became the most important local centre. Before long its new name was given to the territorial division – or shire – over which it held control.

Popular belief has often linked the derivation of Derby with the river Derwent, its Danish *-by* signifying an abode, habitation or village: in this case, the village on the Derwent. However, another interpretation is that it was the abode of the Deoras, descendants of a Viking chieftain called Deor. Either way, the *-by* denoted a place belonging to the initial phase of Danish settlement in England, on eastern and northern lands already under the Vikings' powerful sway. This influx affected Derbyshire mostly between 876-80, settlement also being concentrated in two areas relatively accessible to and from Derby along the former Roman road of Rynkield Street. Names such as Denby, Stainsby and Blingsby near to other *-by* across the county boundary with Nottinghamshire appear to identify the area favoured north of Derby.

Likewise, south of the Trent, the second area extended much more considerably into neighbouring Leicestershire. The Danish place-names here include Smisby, Bretby and Ingleby. Although the last two may recall surviving elements of Britons and Angles respectively amongst the local populace, Ingleby held prominence as the site of a rare Danish cemetery of this period, consisting of over sixty burial mounds – rare because it was so visibly pagan. Some Danish settlers were soon converted to Christianity, but even those who were not usually availed themselves of Christian cemeteries. One mound at Ingleby contained a fragmented sword, a clear reminder that the newcomers remained warriors as well as farmers. Most likely their settlement pattern reflected their organisation into military units headed by warlords based at Derby, the site of which allowed them strategic dominance not only over the five Roman routes converging there from Peak and plain but also over the middle Trent valley, in addition to the Derwent.

Viking raids were instigated from their occupied areas into the un-conquered southern and Western English counties, but King Alfred the Great of Wessex bought peace by appeasing them with money known as Danegeld. So buying time too to build up his army, he proceeded to defeat the Danes in 878 and negotiate a peace treaty restricting their control to England east of Watling Street, which ran from the West Midlands to London; their regions were designated the Danelaw. Alfred's treaty also effectively split Mercia into two, the loyalty of its English sector being ensured by the marriage of his young daughter Ethelfleda to its chief noble, after whose death she ruled in her own right as the 'Lady of Mercia'. Though Derbyshire was wholly within the Danelaw, its nearness to the frontier with Alfred's kingdom made its history bound up with the remnant of Mercia, and that southern Trent area of early Danish settlement a target in the forefront of further hostilities.

The Danes consolidated their strength at Derby, which ranked as one of the Danelaw's five East Midland 'burghs', or fortified towns, each governing its own surrounding territory. Administrative units called 'hundreds' by the Saxons but 'wapentakes' by the Danes formed subdiv-isions within each territory. The area which owed obedience to Derby and ultimately became the county of Derbyshire, receiving its first written mention in 1049, had six: High Peak, Wirksworth (originally jointly forming Hamenstan Wapentake), Appletree, Scarsdale, Morleston and Litchurch, and Repton and Gresley. These remained in existence until the 19th century, but only Wirksworth Wapentake retained its Danish title. This term was therefore an amalgam of Saxon and Viking names, as indeed was Derbyshire itself, since 'shire' originated from Anglo-Saxon 'scir' meaning a district. The meeting-places or 'moots' for the courts of each wapentake can be identified in such obvious instances as Moot Low, Brassington (Wirksworth Wapentake) and Moat Low, Youlgreave (High Peak). In north and mid-Derbyshire, further Danish influence is evident in place-names like Thorpe, Flagg, Holme and Oakerthorpe. The paucity compared with the number of Saxon names by no means implies a lack of domination here, for Danes were installed as lords of existing settlements. An early 10th-century charter refers to a Saxon called Uhtred buying lands from 'the pagans' at Hope and Ashford on the orders of Alfred's successor, King Edward the Elder, an example of territory being peacefully regained from Danes. In the light of previous Peakland invasions, it is hard to imagine that territory in this part of Derbyshire was given up to 'pagans' at all without resistance, and sure enough the area has tales of plundering Vikings being killed

Map 6. Derbyshire hundred divisions. These evolved from the Danish wapentakes, and for several centuries administered a county which has changed relatively little from its original boundaries. Early moot-sites for the northern wapentakes are suggested by place-name evidence.

in ambush, set upon by guard dogs, of a great battle against them near Chapel-en-le-Frith and of the medieval earthwork called Camp Green near Hathersage Church once being a 'Danes Camp'.

However, the real threat to their supremacy in Derbyshire came from the south, from Edward and his sister Ethelfleda, who were determined to win back the Danish part of Mercia. Against this background a second period of building crosses began as some Danes embraced Christianity. But their artwork bore features distinct from the Saxon style, a good example being the broad band of plaitwork on a cross shaft found at Norbury. The remains of a round-shafted cross at Brailsford appropriately depicted a Viking soldier with sword and chain-mail, though, sadly, minus the fabled horned helmet! Crosses were erected too at Derby's former church of St Alkmund's, perhaps to assuage divine vengeance, for according. to legend this saint was slain by Vikings and his body buried here.

Derby represented a rich prize in the designs of Edward and Ethelfleda, but the struggle to recover Danelaw lands rather resembled the movement of a seesaw. The process first concerned Derbyshire in the early years of the 10th century when a small area near Burton-on-Trent returned to Mercian control. By 917, Ethelfleda's troops had fought their way north of the Trent and recaptured Derby under her command, though with heavy loss. Four years after her death in 919, Edward reconquered the Peak, where he ordered a controlling fortress to be built at 'Badecanwyllan', or Bakewell – long held to be Castle Hill, but excavations of its earthworks pointed towards a medieval date. The reign of King Athelstan (925-41) saw the establishment of a royal mint at Derby, a sign of its urban status. The first silver pennies stamped 'Deoraby' gave him the title 'King of the Saxons'. But when the Danes reoccupied the town, its coins bore the name of their leader, Anlaf. After they had once more been defeated in 937, Athelstan's inscribed title became 'King of All Britain'. During the reign of Ethelred (978-1016) the royal title on Derby coins was more accurately 'King of the English'. However, as his alternative title of 'the Unready' (Ethelred No-Counsel, probably a play on his name which meant 'noble counsel') indicates, his weak and stormy rule was beset by further Danish invasions. Some coins then minted at Derby are thought to have a raven design on the reverse side – the emblem carried on Viking banners – and so probably represented Danegeld. Despite such efforts to placate yet keep them away, Danish kings succeeded him and the Saxon royal line was not restored until Edward the Confessor in 1042.

Although nationally unsettled, the late 10th and early 11th centuries marked a further period of church-building in Derbyshire, the local pre-eminence of its county town clearly shown by the existence around this time of six parishes: St Alkmund's and St Werburgh's, already mentioned, plus All Saints', St Michael's, St Mary's and St Peter's. Repton's re-emergence to aspire to something of its former glory belonged

Soldier on the shaft of Brailsford's Danish cross

Athelstan silver penny minted at 'Deoraby'

45

both to these and later centuries, as we shall see in Chapter VII. Amongst other churches still bearing traces of late Saxon work is Mugginton, which has as its close companion an ancient yew tree believed to be older than the church itself. In pre-Christian times, the yew was regarded as a sacred tree, symbolising the soul's immortality in the after-life, a notion subsequently in obvious keeping with a church setting. The age of Derbyshire's famous 'Darley Yew' in the churchyard at Darley Dale remains inconclusive, sometimes given as over two thousand years old, sometimes as less than a thousand. But the discovery of pre-Christian burials both here and at Mugginton backs up the view that these were already hallowed sites before the advent of Christianity.

In the medieval era about to dawn in the mid-11th century, yew trees were also to prove especially significant in the making of longbows, and many more of today's churches around the county were to be erected, representing a variety of Romanesque and Gothic styles. The pattern of settlement established in Derbyshire before Britons, Anglo-Saxons and Danes in its population merged under the oppression of the Norman Conquest was also largely to stand the test of time.

Coin of Ethelred's reign from the Derby mint, the reverse depicting the Hand of Providence between Alpha and Omega

VI Conquerors and Conquered

A stoop; a stride; a grave; two caves; two wells; a moss; a cross; a chair; a table; a leap and even a pair of picking rods: in this curious-sounding list of features in north Derbyshire, there are in fact only two 'odd men out' – the grave and one of the wells, named after Little John. The rest all belong to Robin Hood. There is little wonder that an area so strong in traditions and folklore became as closely linked as its Yorkshire and Nottinghamshire neighbours with the great greenwood hero and the best known of his Merry Men, said to be a bowman from Hathersage. The Middle Ages marking 'Merrie England' were hardly so for most of its people, perhaps least of all at times for those who dwelt in the 'Robin Hood Country'. After the Norman Conquest in 1066, the newcomers succeeded where previous conquerors had failed, in swiftly and effectively subjugating the Peak.

Robin Hood on an inn sign in the hamlet named after him near Chesterfield

Assumptions have been made that, as before, lowland Derbyshire was more easily subdued. Examples cited of co-operation between new order and old include the rare achievement of the pre-Conquest Lord of Brailsford, Elfin, in retaining his lands afterwards and that of Saxon and Norman masons working together to build the southern Trent church at Stanton-by-Bridge, which bears evidence of an architectural 'overlap' period. Yet in the Domesday Book of 1086, the impact of conquerors upon conquered throughout the county during the early restive years is sadly evident. The tracts of Derbyshire classified as 'waste' may partly have resulted from the Normans' scorched-earth method of quelling the northern English risings in 1069. The well-known village of Hartington was amongst those in the White Peak probably then destroyed. Although Domesday Derby retained its royal mint and six churches, its 103 desolated dwellings showed that the town had suffered and sunk into decline, much loss of its menfolk in 1066 due to battles outside the county against both Norman and defeated Viking invaders: the 243 leading townsmen, or burgesses, and 14 mills of Edward the Confessor's reign had diminished to 100 and 10 respectively when the Norman survey was compiled. Whether Peakland or lowland communities, county manors revealed similar trends: Horsley, north of Derby, 'in the time of King Edward was worth 100 shillings, now 60 shillings' and at Little John's Hathersage the equivalent values were 60 shillings reduced to thirty.

The Book also detailed many Derbyshire villages as 'berewicks' –

these were the old Saxon settlements subsidiary to a manor. The royal manor of Hope held sway over seven berewicks, including Aston, Edale and Tideswell, and was the site of an early Norman fortification close to the church. This defence most likely protected the manor house and typified a new element in the construction of strongholds, for the estates were administered from behind private fortifications. As time went on, the Normans progressed from small defences such as this and castles of earth and timber to overawe the subjected populace with castles of stone and mighty keeps built of walls up to fifteen feet thick – of which Duffield Castle, once with one of England's largest keeps, must have been a fine example. The county's other major medieval castles were sited for varying periods at Bakewel!, Bolsover, Bretby, Castle Gresley, Castleton, Codnor, Derby, Horeston, Mackworth, Melbourne, Pilsbury and Pinxton.

Such outward signs of Norman authority well matched the political and economic domination they imposed over the whole country, strengthening the established manorial system by grafting onto it a rigid military hierarchy – a system known as feudalism, which had gradually developed in Dark Age Europe as an arrangement for creating order out of the post-Roman chaos. Its social structure was based on a strong personal bond between an overlord and his vassals, a dependence often transcending ties of kinship, in which the latter were provided with estates from the former's lands in return for 'fees' comprising military services and dutiful homage bound by sacred oath. Under the Danelaw, a social class of freehold tenants called sokemen had emerged, who farmed manor smallholdings in exchange for fixed rents and non-military services to their lord. Under the Normans, they formed the lowest rung of military vassals. Beneath them were the majority of the population, unfree manorial appendages who worked the land held by the lord for his own use. Made up of villeins (farmers with their own smallholdings), bordars (farm labourers) and cottagers (lower peasants with no land entitlement) – and their families – they could be punished, sold, given away or dragged off on military campaigns as the lord decided. Villeins at Matlock and Wensley were amongst many in medieval Derbyshire recorded as gifts or items of sale, usually with land and chattels. Heading the social scale, the lord of all lords was the king himself from whom the successive levels of nobility, gentry, esquires and freemen ultimately all held their land. William the Conqueror therefore significantly controlled his new realm by granting power over large areas to his own sworn supporters. In Derbyshire he kept for himself Derby borough and over forty of Edward's former manors, including Hope, making William Peveril the foremost Norman in the Peak with 20 northern manors and Henry de Ferrers the county's chief landowner with 114 manors. From Norman knights also rewarded for serving him are descended several well-known Derbyshire families, such as Meynell, Vernon, Fitzherbert, Foljambe, Eyre and Curzon.

Brass of Sir John Foljambe, Tideswell church

48

13. Dale Abbey: destroyers of monastic buildings after the Dissolution are said to have left the east end of the church until last, feeling appropriate dread as they approached the high altar. This may have been the case at Dale, where the wall containing the east window is the only fragment left upstanding. Morley church contains much stained glass from this once-beautiful Premonstratensian abbey.

14. Derby Cathedral from Irongate. The church of All Saints became a cathedral in 1927, exactly 400 years after its fine perpendicular tower was built.

15. Entrance to Repton School, founded 1557, through the medieval priory gateway. The former priory buildings still retain original features.

16. Etwall Almshouses, erected and endowed in the mid-Tudor period by Sir John Port, founder of Repton School, for eight poor people. The wrought iron gates, fashioned by Robert Bakewell, stood originally at Etwall Hall.

17. Tissington Hall, manor house of the FitzHerberts, dating from 1590.

Early Norman church, Tissington.

19. (*above*) Somersall Hall, Somersall Herbert.

20. (*below*) Sudbury Hall, one of England's finest Stuart mansions and the home, early in Queen Victoria's reign, of the Dowager Queen Adelaide.

Map 7. Aspects of secular life in medieval Derbyshire: royal hunting forests, castles, lead-mining and markets. The small number of centrally-placed markets may partly account for the considerable importance of those at Derby, Chesterfield and Wirksworth.

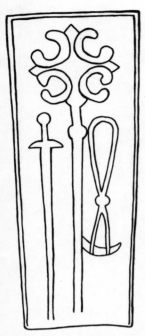

Tombstone of a Duffield Frith chief forester, Wirksworth church, showing his badges of office

Because feudal ties determining property ownership were so essentially military and male-dominated, the status of women in post Conquest England became more subservient. Even though in the later Middle Ages payments of rent largely replaced the duty-bound military services, a husband's automatic legal right to his own wife's property was only repealed in 1882. In the Royal Forest of the High Peak established by the Conqueror, women could attain the usually hereditary titles of the forest officials, paying the Crown a fee for the privilege, but were barred from carrying out their office – that right too passed to husbands. A 'forest' was then synonymous with an extensive area set apart as royal hunting ground (a 'chase' sufficed for humbler folk) and embraced in this case not only woodland but much of Derbyshire's wasteland, comprising Dark Peak moors and mountains where deer, wild boars and until Tudor times even wolves roamed freely. A large expanse of Peak Forest lay within the parish of Hope and so had already seen Saxon royal hunts. But here, as in other English forests, the Normans introduced strict laws concerning the king's vert and venison (vegetation and deer) severely enforced by special courts and officials including verderers and foresters, serving under a chief bailiff.

From the 12th century, Peak Forest occupied most of north-west Derbyshire, its boundaries following the rivers Goyt, Etherow, Derwent, Bradwell and Wye. It was split into three wards: Hopedale, Longdendale and Campagna. Farther south, the smaller Duffield Frith had four: Belper, Colebrook, Duffield and Hulland. Sherwood Forest also reached partly into east Derbyshire around Pinxton. Each forest had its own laws and punishments, amongst them fines, castration, loss of eyes or limbs and even death, for poaching offences such as 'back-bear' (found carrying away a slain deer), 'stable-stand' (caught ready to shoot at deer or let hounds off their leash) and the more self-explanatory 'bloody-hand'.

Peveril Castle, on a precipitous site above Castleton, was originally built soon after 1068 by William Peveril to administer Peak Forest, of which he was the first bailiff. Gruesome tales evoking its penal role underline how cheaply earthly existence was regarded in medieval times: in one curious incident, a group of poachers imprisoned here were freed by the castle's constables and ordered to appear before the forest court, but when they did so he accused two of having broken prison and decapitated them. In trouble himself then for this summary justice, he incurred a fine of 10 marks for their escape! Even the Peverils came to grief in 1153 when William Peveril IV forfeited all his estates to the Crown, not for transgressing forest laws, but allegedly poisoning the Earl of Chester. However, Richard Vernon, heir of Haddon, and his brother lost the family manor to their cousin after being outlawed and banished for killing 'two stags and three bissas'. Following Henry VII's reign (1154-89), during which England's monarch received the submission of the Scottish King at Peveril Castle and the stone keep

Peveril Castle, nowadays featured on the badge of the Peak National Park

was added, the crime of venison trespass became something of a vogue despite the risks. In 1250, the indictment of an official called Henry de Elton concerned his taking over two thousand deer during his six years of office, and the law also caught up with other chief men, including the 5th Earl of Derby (the de Ferrers family had gained this title after the Battle of the Standard in 1138) and the Bishop of Chester. In 1264, the 6th Earl of Derby was twice accused of illegal hunting.

This young man, Robert de Ferrers, made a far worse nuisance of himself within the county in 1266, however, when, after being forgiven for his part in Simon de Montfort's rebellion against Henry III, he returned to the family seat at Duffield and began to arm his Derbyshire tenantry, clearly intending to rebel again. Royalist troops sent to deal with him initially intercepted a contingent of Yorkshire rebels at Chesterfield, whom the Earl rushed to support, only to be defeated in the fierce ensuing battle. He was captured hiding amongst bags of wool in Chesterfield Church, apparently betrayed by a girl whose lover had been killed in the battle, having first been compelled, like the Earl's own feudal underlings, to join the rebels. Although his life was spared, all his manors were confiscated and settled on Edmund, Earl of Lancaster, later becoming part of the Duchy of Lancaster under its first Duke, John of Gaunt. Traditionally, Duffield Castle was totally despoiled by victorious troops after the encounter at Chesterfield.

The prime object of de Montfort's rising, for a 'People's Parliament', became reality in Edward I's reign (1272-1307) and the first recorded Derbyshire representatives were two knights, Henry de Kniveton and Giles de Meynell and, for Derby, two burgesses John de la Cornere and Ralph de Makeyen. It was under Edward's auspices too that an inquisition held at Ashbourne in spring 1288 formally recognised the ancient laws still controlling local lead-mining today from 'time immemorable'. Derbyshire was the only county specified as lead-producing in Domesday Book, with mines at Ashford, Bakewell, Crich, Matlock and Wirksworth. By the 1170s the area around Castleton and Hope was also in production and one reason for strengthening Peveril Castle in this decade (its keep cost £180 to build in 1175-6) was to govern the royal mines. Also at this time, Castleton itself was laid out, surrounded by an earthen rampart.

The industry's special jargon and unique customs and laws have added much to local culture. The Barmote Courts alluded to in Chapter IV were set up, each with a steward, barmaster, deputy and jurymen, to enforce its time-honoured practices in both High and Low Peak regions, the latter having a single court at Wirksworth, where it still meets twice yearly. (Barmasters also acted as coroners of the mines.) At Ashbourne, the inquisition confirmed all miners' right without permission or paying of money to 'dig or delve' for ore anywhere in the Peakland mineral area, termed the King's Field, except churches, houses, gardens and orchards. Once a prospector had located a lead

Lead miners' standard dish, Wirksworth

51

vein or 'rake' the first dish of ore was payable to the landowner to free the mine. After the barmaster and two jurymen had staked our two meers of ground (a meer varied between 27 and 32 yards according to locality), the miner gained title and possession of the mine, could work it unhindered and have space for leaving waste material. On each meer's extent, a 'stow' or windlass had to stand, hand-propelled to bring miner and mineral to the surface, but also signifying ownership. A mine marked out wrongly was liable to forfeit and possession of one not worked to be 'nicked' or assigned to another owner – a term now in general colloquial use!

Duties were payable to the Crown and Church for every 'lot' or 13th dish of ore plus the extra 'cope' amounting to fourpence in the High Peak and sixpence around Wirksworth for every lode or nine dishes. The Tudor standard dish in Wirksworth's Moot Hall holds about sixty-two pounds of ore; a standard measure for the High Peak, formerly at Monyash, was slightly larger. Wirksworth miners also paid every 40th dish as tithes to their rector. The serious crime of stealing ore was punished by fines for the first and second offences, but proof of a third led to the culprit being fixed to a stow with a knife through his hand and left either to die or release himself by amputating his hand. Survival also entailed the loss of his freedom and mining privileges for life.

Bole Hill near Wirksworth takes its name from the early method of ore-smelting in hollows called boles on hills facing a prevailing westerly wind. The long-distance trade for lead was wholly reliant on its transportation by sturdy packhorse trains negotiating Peak country along many nowadays popular walkers' trails. Medieval waymarks include Edale Cross (restored 1610) on the Peak Forest boundary and, north-west of Kinder, Abbot's Chair which, being on Monks Road, doubly recalls the long tenure of 80 Longendale acres by the Welsh abbey of Basingwerk. Further ecclesiastical influence is evident in the name of nearby Chapel-en-le-Frith (the forest chapel of Duffield Frith was at Belper) and, mostly in the southern Peak, numerous isolated farmsteads called granges: the Roman Roystone and Saxon Benty Granges of previous chapters saw medieval use as sheep farms, from which their monastic owners produced wool, the mainstay of England's trade with Europe and chief commodity handled by the powerful Derby Merchants' Company which emerged in the 13th century.

Local trade was encouraged by markets and fairs established under royal charter and often linked to religious festivals and feast-days, possibly a survival from ancient pagan practice. Although Derby and the 13th-century borough of Chesterfield were each granted charters in 1204, records tell of markets there at least forty years before. Other early charters included: Hartington (1203), Castleton (1222), Tideswell (1251), Alfreton, Ilkeston and Sandiacre (1252), Bakewell (1254), Ashbourne (1257), Pleasley (1275), Glossop (1290) and Wirksworth (1306). The majority were close to the county boundary, and across the centre stretched a market 'chain' from north-west to south-east – near the route of the prehistoric Portway.

Bridge-chapels such as the one restored on St Mary's Bridge, Derby, served travellers' spiritual needs, for indeed amid the transient journey of earthly life and events, religion then shone indispensably for all, reassuringly constant especially during the century of social upheaval after the Black Death in 1349. Its depopulation of Derbyshire is reflected in the situation at Ashford, where lead-mining ceased for lack of labour. Demand for labour was generally far outweighing its supply and so the tenantry who survived the plague could secure high wages and low rents, sometimes – as at Walton-on-Trent – without any service. The feudal ties began to break down, despite instances such as the fining of 120 Morleston labourers in 1358 for taking excessive wages. Changing times were eventually to reduce the majority of the county's medieval castles to decayed traces of former pride. Yet at Ballidon, one of the few Derbyshire villages to be deserted through depopulation then, the Norman church still stands.

Angry fox and its reflection on the tomb of Sir Nicholas Knive-ton, Mugginton church: said to symbolize his cunning in warfare

VII · The Age of Faith

*Medieval hermitage,
Harthill Moor*

The narrow road leading from Tideswell to the Peakland hamlet of Wheston winds steeply past the base of a medieval wayside cross and, in less than another mile, a complete cross, with the Birth of Christ depicted on one side, his Crucifixion on the other – a rare surviving example of which many once existed within the county. Perhaps not surprisingly, in the Middle Ages this route was named Crossgate and its guiding landmarks doubtless prompted passing mortals, rich or poor, to reflect upon the future well-being of their souls. 'The Age of Faith', as the centuries from the 11th to the 15th are also known, was a time when religion not only pervaded spiritual and secular aspects of people's lives but the Church was a power to be reckoned with.

There are varied visual symbols inherited from those days, amongst them the hermit's cave on Harthill Moor with an imposing cross and altar carved into its gritstone walls; a Pieta of the Blessed Virgin Mary and her crucified Son in Breadsall church; the tiny 'architectural gem' of Steetley chapel and the Lamb of God, triumphant over the forces of evil on the Norman tympanum at Parwich church. In the church at Tideswell itself, a Latin inscription on the tomb of Sir Sampson Meverell bears a simple message in translation: 'He who has persevered to the very end shall be saved'. Another, in English, asks for prayers for all Christian souls and 'especiall the soule whose bons resten under this stone'. When the fighting qualities which made this Derbyshire knight a hero at battles such as Agincourt (1415) were allowed to spill over into domestic disputes, he earned a certain notoriety. Yet, according to his epitaph, in later life he entered the service of John Stafford, Archbishop of Canterbury, and 'soe endurring in great worship departed from all worldly service unto the mercy of Our Lord Jesu Christ . . . '.

Of a similar quarrelsome nature but also mindful of his salvation was Sir Thomas Wendesley, buried at Bakewell, whose memorial effigy there was sculpted in alabaster quarried at Chellaston, as were many impressive tombs of this period. His 'shameful trespasses' included an incident in which a man had his right hand cut off. In 1384, however, Wendesley was recorded as being the patron of one Roger de Upton, the new prior of Breadsall. The errant knight had probably gained this privilege by some specific act of endowment to the priory. After his death in battle in 1403, his widow became a nun.

It was in atonement for sin, or to seek a place in heaven, or purely

Steetley Chapel

from a deep religious faith that men and women of high rank endowed monasteries with land, in return for which Masses would be said for their souls. For love of God, too, people were prepared to dedicate their lives to Him, forsaking the pleasures of the outside world for a regime of penances, fasting and prayer within the confines of a religious house. However easily we may think of these unarmed monks and nuns as pious recluses who left the shaping of secular medieval England to knights in shining armour or the lords in their grim stone castles, in reality by the 13th century the monasteries owned about a third of the land. If we consider that another third of England was then waste (mostly marsh or, as in Derbyshire, barren moorland), an idea of the Church's strength becomes clearer.

Some religious communities became very wealthy indeed, but as individuals their members were required to relinquish all personal property. In Derbyshire, as elsewhere in England, the monasteries consisted of both abbeys and priories, the difference between them being one of status – a priory was usually smaller. The county also had a preceptory of Yeaveley, belonging to an order of soldier monks called the Knights Hospitaller, or Knights of St John. It was founded in the reign of Richard I (1189-99) and one of its main duties was to help provide finance for the actively military section of the order, whose presence in charge of all the medical arrangements of this king's army had played a crucial role on the Third Crusade. Together with a hermitage at Yeaveley, the founder, Ralph Foun, gave lands, waters, woods and mills to the new establishment, stipulating that it should receive him clad in the habit of the Hospitallers whenever he wished, either in sickness or in health.

The distinctive habit worn by each different order immediately set them apart from the secular world. Vows of celibacy and of obedience to the acknowledged head of the community were also inherent in the monastic ideal. Otherwise, the way each day was lived to the glory of God depended very much on the rules of the various orders. The Benedictines, who emphasised hard work as well as prayer, the Cluniacs who devoted most of their time to church services, the Dominicans, noted for their preaching, and two orders of canons, the Augustinians and the stricter Premonstratensians, all peopled the monasteries of Derbyshire.

As mentioned in Chapter IV, the county's earliest religious house was founded at Repton long before the Norman Conquest. Close to the site of that ancient abbey destroyed by the Danes, a parish church of considerable size was built. The Domesday survey described it as having two priests, a distinction shared only by Bakewell of all the other Derbyshire churches. Dedicated to the Mercian prince, St Wystan, it was granted around 1160 to the canons of Calke Priory by Matilda, Dowager Countess of Chester and Lady of the manor of Repton, on condition that Calke should become dependent on the priory she intended to found at Repton.

Repton Priory gatehouse

55

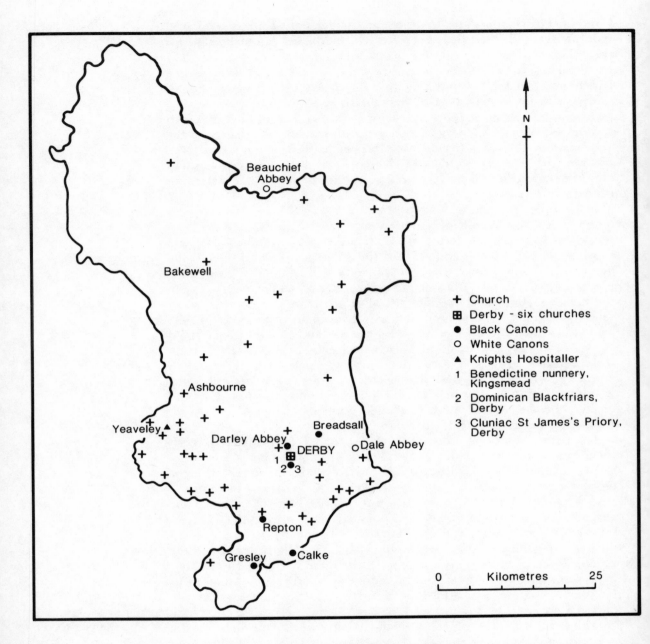

Map 8. Aspects of the Age of Faith: Derbyshire churches identified in Domesday, and medieval religious houses.

56

By 1172, the second monastery in this ancient Christian centre had become the daughter-house of the first to be founded after the Conquest. The priory of Augustinian canons at Calke is known to have been in existence before 1100, when a nearby Nottinghamshire church was committed to its care, provided that a canon who was a priest would celebrate daily Mass there. Since all the monks of this order were also priests, they could act in that capacity in churches given to them and even their own abbey and priory churches could be attended by the laity. Their wearing of a black habit earned them the name of Black Canons. Eventually, Calke became incorporated with Repton Priory and the newer foundation in its turn echoed back to the days of its Saxon predecessor, for it had a shrine to the most famous of its Mercian monks, St Guthlac, which made it a place of pilgrimage. A relic, in the form of the saint's small sanctus-bell, was attributed with the power of curing headache when applied to a pilgrim's head.

'Ave Maria' design on a medieval tile from Repton

The bells of another Augustinian priory tolled the daily round of prayer at Gresley, a few miles away, from the early 12th century. Founded by William de Gresley, lord of the nearby castle, its much-restored church of St George served also then, as it does now, as the village church, the canons themselves using the chancel as their chapel. Their next possession came on the north-west side of Derby in 1137, when a burgess called Towyne founded the priory of St Helen's. Though its name lives on in the street where it was originally sited, this small house of canons had little time to flourish: in the same way that Repton grew out of, and then took over Calke, so the richest abbey in Derbyshire was the offspring of St Helen's.

That abbey was Darley, situated by the banks of the river Derwent two miles north of Derby. Its favourable setting resulted from the benefactions of its two founders, Robert de Ferrers, 2nd Earl of Derby, and Hugh, Dean of Derby. The former had given lands to the Church for the purpose of building an abbey; the latter offered the prior of St Helen's control of these and the patronage of St Peter's church in Derby if he would erect an abbey at Darley. The prior, Albinus, became its first abbot *c.* 1151 and by 1160 St Helen's was totally subject to it. Also under its jurisdiction came the priory of Benedictine nuns founded that year in King's Meadow (or Kingsmead), the hospital of St Leonard's for lepers, Derby School and three of the town's churches. 'Perpetual alms' came too in abundance from other parts of the county, making the abbots of Darley men of power and prestige for almost four centuries. The abbey church was completed during Albinus's rule and would have resembled in style the large Norman church at Melbourne, nine miles away, where a royal manor had been granted to the Bishops of Carlisle in 1135 and, because of Scottish raids into England's border country, often provided the setting for their court.

The dedication of the former Derbyshire abbey of Beauchief to St Thomas à Becket is said to have been in expiation for his murder, its

57

founder Robert FitzRanulph, Lord of Alfreton, being one of his alleged assassins. But the story has been refuted. When the abbey was brought into being in 1175, the reason stated by FitzRanulph himself was 'for the health of the soul of King Henry II and for the health of the souls of his children, and for the health of his own soul, and the souls of his relations, and for the soul of his father, and his mother, and all his ancestors'. The Premonstratensian canons who dwelt there commemorated him every 9 September. This order wore white habits and so were known as the White Canons.

Like several other religious houses, including Darley Abbey and the nunnery in Derby, Beauchief was also dedicated to the Blessed Virgin Mary. Such was the depth of devotion to her that England was regarded as 'Mary's dowry' and images of her as Our Lady of Pity, with the body of her dead Son in her arms, were often represented in medieval churches. Repton had 'an image of our lady in our lady of petys chapel' and the churchwardens' accounts for All Saints', Derby, mention an entry for five tapers 'before the mary of pety'. At Breadsall, where the last Derbyshire priory of Black Canons was founded before 1266, the village church had a priest, in addition to the rector, whose special duty it was to celebrate Mass at the altar of Our Lady and for whose support an endowment of land called St Mary's Meadow and half an acre of arable land was made. The men who centuries ago said Mass watched over by the figure of Mary still present in the church were named locally 'our ladye priest'.

But if ever an abbey could claim to have a heavenly-inspired setting as the reason for its dedication to the Blessed Virgin, it was the abbey of Dale, the second house of White Canons in Derbyshire. Legend says that a devout baker of Derby saw a vision of the Virgin, who praised his good deeds and desired him to abandon all his worldly goods and serve God through solitude and prayer in a place called Deepdale. Total obedience brought him to this still-secluded valley six miles east of Derby, where he made a hermitage in the sandstone cliffs. Later the local Lord, Ralph FitzGeremund, bestowed upon him the site of the hermitage with adjacent lands for his support, and on the site of the eventual abbey church he built an oratory with shelter adjoining.

Dale Abbey in fact came about through the repeated attempts of FitzGeremund's Anglo-Norman descendants to perpetuate this holy place. At the fourth bid, his granddaughter Matilda and her husband, Geoffrey de Salicosa Mara, were at last successful, for they endowed the abbey with the extensive nearby lands of Stanley Park. The story of its foundation was subsequently written down by a canon called Thomas de Musca, as related to him by Matilda in her old age. Its final opening was dated 15 August 1204 – the Feast of the Assumption of the Blessed Virgin Mary.

While Premonstratensian abbeys such as Dale flourished in their well-endowed but solitary places, other orders preferred to set up

Norman font with holy water stoup, Youlgreave church

58

their communities solely in towns, yet spurned the idea of becoming landowners and relied instead on the alms of the public to whom they ministered. The Dominicans were an order of friar-preachers who appeared in England in the early 13th century, becoming known as Blackfriars. The only link between their Derby priory and the county's larger abbeys was its naming after Mary. Henry III, Edward I and Edward II all gave money for the building of their church in the parish of St Werburgh's. The priory entrance was on Friar Gate. Nearer the town centre stood the Cluniac priory of St James's, which also remained small, its monks thus freer of the worldly pressures of wealth which began to afflict the greater monasteries.

Medieval font of local lead, Ashover church

Inevitably, the occupants of those which had acquired vast estates became ensnared in the problems of their management and administration. One Ash Grange, Monyash, served the dual role of sheep farm and house of correction for wayward monks of Roche Abbey, South Yorkshire! As for Darley Abbey, stories of scandal there were so widespread in Richard II's reign (1377-99) that the king himself assumed control for four years. Two centuries afterwards, the noted antiquarian and traveller, William Camden, summed up the monasteries' years of decline: 'there were never more certain indications and glorious monuments of Christian piety and devotion to God than were those . . . however, it came to pass that in a loose age some rank weeds ran up too fast, which required rooting out'.

Rank weeds there may have been, but when it came to rooting them out the process caused genuine sorrow amongst people of all classes in Derbyshire. Undoubtedly, the monastic revival or 'the Age of Faith' had lost its momentum by the 14th and 15th centuries, when very few new foundations were made elsewhere and none at all in this county. However, new adornments to existing structures and some building work still went on. The stained glass windows which add to the beauty of Morley church were originally installed in the cloisters of Dale in the late 15th century and years before, in 1453, an agreement had been reached between John Stathum of Morley and Thomas, Prior of Breadsall, by which the priory undertook, in consideration of a gift of seven marks for the priory church roof and windows, to say an annual Mass for various members of the Stathum family on the feast of the 11,000 Virgins (21 October). The windows removed from Dale to Morley after the abbey's closure, by coincidence, include one depicting the legend of that feast day. These and other features, chiefly stonework, owe their initial survival to the foresight of Francis Pole, who purchased them when Dale was dismantled.

The scanty remains left at Deepdale bear silent witness that the Dissolution of the monasteries under Henry VIII fell with a heavy hand in Derbyshire. Since only Darley had an annual income of more than £200, the smaller priories met their end in the first round of suppression in 1536. Dale and Repton managed to buy exemption, but that only

59

helped them for two or three years, when Darley also was dissolved. Its very thorough destruction ordered soon after was a measure of the fear amongst Henry's commissioners of the local opposition to their schemes. The priory church at Repton was demolished in a single day, its new secular owner, Gilbert Thacker, having declared he 'would destroy the nest, for fear the birds should build therein again'.

Cromford Bridge Chapel, suppressed at the Reformation

At Buxton, the shrine to St Anne fell victim at the same time as the monasteries, but preventing the sick and disabled from outwardly honouring their patron saint did not deter them from continuing their 'superstitious' pilgrimages to its well in their thousands, hoping that its healing water would restore them with a miraculous cure. Despite official government policy to reform the religious practices of 'the Age of Faith', in fact it never really died in Derbyshire but, like streams and rivers in some of the White Peak's limestone dales, disappeared underground only to re-surface farther on. The Dissolution transferred into willing lay hands ecclesiastic lands, goods and chattels, but not all local inhabitants were willing and, as will be seen in chapters to come, the deeply intrinsic adherence to the Church of Rome was to re-emerge again and again.

VIII   A Derbyshire Manor

'At Tissington, FitzHerbert's village, we saw the springs adorned with garlands.' This first written record of Derbyshire well-dressing came from a visitor in 1758 to the southern Peakland village where every year this beautiful custom begins on Ascension Day. The same admirer went on to emphasise not only its antiquity but its profoundly religious character, involving the ceremonial consecration of each well. Already, Tissington had been 'FitzHerbert's village' for almost three centuries, nowadays for more than five and nearer nine through its lord's female ancestry. In every sense it is a classic English village, its church and manor house being focal points amid an ensemble of great charm. Behind the church, a small fortification similar to that at Hope remains from early feudal days.

Village scene, Tissington

The FitzHerberts of this originally Saxon manor are of a different lineage from the FitzHerberts of Norbury who figured so prominently in later Derbyshire history. According to medieval documents, the spelling of Tissington too – and even its pronunciation – varied, between its present form and Tystyngton, Tistenton, Tiscenton and Tiscington, leading to divergent ideas on whether its name is derived from 'the farmstead of' Tisa, Tidsige or Titstan. Domesday Book contained yet another version – Tizinctun – and detailed the manor amongst those of Henry de Ferrers in Wirksworth Wapentake. No church was mentioned, but other assets included: four carucates of land (each being an old measure, averaging *c.* 120 acres, for the amount of land one plough could till in a season); 12 villeins and eight bordars with four ploughs; a mill worth three shillings; meadowland of 30 acres and woodland one league long and half a mile wide. Its pre-Conquest value of £4 had fallen to 40 shillings.

Ownership of Tissington passed from the de Ferrers to the Savage family in Henry I's reign (1100-35) and the church of St Mary's erected on a small eminence to serve the tiny community retains some of its early 12th-century appearance. The solid Norman tower typifies those of other village churches in this part of Derbyshire close to Dovedale; a fine Norman doorway with tympanum above and two side pillars reputedly worn down by arrow-sharpening allows entry to the inner sanctum where further rounded Romanesque features include the chancel arch and almost tub-like font, which sports a curious assemblage of carvings, comprising human figures, a bird and animals of uncertain

Norman tympanum, Tissington church

61

species, one of the latter apparently eating its own tail while another consumes a man – no doubt appropriate symbolism in a village bounding on the royal hunting forest of Duffield Frith! For centuries, St Mary's was a chapelry of All Saints', Bradbourne, which in 1205 formed an endowment along with its chapels in Tissington, Atlow, Ballidon and Brassington to the Augustinian priory of Dunstable, Bedfordshire. The priory's annals recorded receipt in 1223 of the first crop from the two chapelries of Ballidon and Tissington as tithes, and in 1227 the recovery for its own use of a half-portion of the tithes after the death of one 'J. de Tattenhulle' to whom the portion had seemingly been leased.

Grassy mounds and hollows in fields adjacent to Ballidon church mark the village eventually abandoned there after the Black Death of the mid-14th century. But at Tissington, which local tradition claims alone escaped the terrible devastation of this plague, the three-sided earthwork slightly north of the church once enfolded the medieval manor house. Being situated above spring level, it was probably not a moated site such as existed, for instance, at Ashford and Fenny Bentley.

The last male heir of the Savages died in 1259, after which the manor was divided between his two daughters and co-heiresses: Phillippa, who married Hugh de Meynell, steward of the 5th Earl of Derby, and Lucy, who married Thomas de Edensor. Subsequent documents showed that the Meynell moiety, or half, was 'held in chief', but in 1272 one 'Richard de Edensor de Tissington' was obviously in residence. King Henry III received the homage of Hugh in 1260 for the lands acquired through Phillippa. Although no specifically unsavoury events appear to be recorded for medieval Tissington, she thought fit in 1275 to claim the right of erecting gallows there. From her elder son Sir William Meynell, who died in 1314, the moiety passed by the marriage of his fifth-generation descendant Joan (c. 1390s) to Sir Thomas Clinton, then through their daughter Anne to Robert Francis of Foremark and finally through their daughter Cicely to Nicholas FitzHerbert, second son of the Lord of Somersal Herbert. The Edensor moiety, meanwhile, passed by marriage to the Harthill family and then the Cockaynes, but in Elizabethan times was bought by Francis FitzHerbert, thus reuniting the manor.

Tissington's traditional deliverance from the Black Death, said to have carried off more than half of Derbyshire's population, was ascribed to God's special mercy and the abundance and purity of the water issuing from its five wells. In consequence, each well was dressed with flowers and blessed in thanksgiving, from 1350, on the Feast of Christ's Ascension into heaven – this, then, is the conjectured origin of one of Derbyshire's unique customs, or more likely a revival within Christian procession and prayer of a much older practice. For a water supply such as Tissington's was already a great cause for thanksgiving in the fast-draining White Peak, a tendency accentuated in 'the Age of Faith' with the widespread veneration of holy wells such as St Anne's at Buxton.

The vivid transparency of the water at Tissington rivals in brightness the Dove and Wye, and added to this quality is a constantly mild temperature throughout the year. The Reformation doubtless halted for a time the reverential rites accorded to this precious commodity, but the water, which has never been known itself to cease, 'rescued' the villagers once more during a severe drought in 1615. This date for the reappearance of well-dressing, in spite of strong objections from the extreme Protestants known as Puritans, is again based on tradition but the Youlgreave parish registers establish as fact the drought that year when 'no rayne fell upon the earth . . . so that the greatest part of this land was burnt upp'.

With the passage of time, the annual dressings at the Hall, Town, Coffin (so called from its shape), Hand's (named after the family who dwelt in the adjacent farm for 200 years) and Yew Tree Wells evolved into their present art-form of lower-mosaics, usually of biblical scenes made up of petals and other natural materials pressed onto a layer of clay, and mounted on a wooden frame. Only sight of them when fresh can truly appreciate their beauty. Nowadays the custom flourishes in 20 Peakland towns and villages at varying dates in its May-September season.

A 13th-century treatise concluded that the optimum distance for travel to market then was seven miles. Within this distance of Tissington were medieval markets at Ashbourne, Hartington and Wirksworth. The route to Ashbourne, the nearest, via Fenny Bentley was certainly in existence by the 18th century, but a more definitely ancient way there lay across on the western side of the Wash Brook valley between Tissington and neighbouring Thorpe. This route, Spend Lane, led past Hamston Hill from Moat Low, one of the three pre-Conquest moot sites for Wirksworth Wapentake (as noted in Chapter V, originally part of *Hamenstan* Wapentake). Interestingly enough, a 'Hamestan Waye' existed at Carsington, probably making for Moot Low at Brassington and so forming part of the Tissington villagers' route to Wirksworth market.

However, although generally medieval agriculture became slowly more orientated towards producing food for market, the need for each rural community remained very much one of self-sufficiency. At Tissington, this situation seems to have prevailed long after the Middle Ages, incorporating too a requisite mixture of village tradesfolk such as a blacksmith, butcher, shoemaker, stonemason and wheelwright. Even now, the approach to the village beyond Tissington Gates along a tree-shaded avenue rather resembles a private drive.

Like the lowland settlements, those in the White Peak below one thousand feet mostly practised the conventional three open-field system of arable farming, each field in turn being allowed to lie fallow for a year. Often, where arable land later became pasturage, the medieval ploughing in long, thin strips for the crops of individual families has left wave-like undulations called 'ridge and furrow', which is much in evidence near Tissington. Another link with the past, a reminder of the

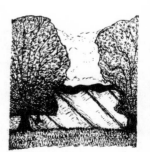

Medieval ridge and furrow from Tissington's lime avenue approach

woodland mentioned in Domesday Book, is the name 'Tissington Wood Farm' south-west of the village.

Bradbourne and its chapelries were served by secular clergy instead of Black Canons from the 14th century (a previous monastic incumbent had been accused of keeping a concubine, amongst other irregularities!) Residing at Tissington, where Dunstable Priory granted them all the tithes of corn, hay and lambs, the secular vicars received also the tithes from mills throughout the parish. After the Reformation, the FitzHerberts of Tissington belonged to the Derbyshire gentry who adhered to the Church of England. Their several memorials in the village church include one to Francis FitzHerbert, who after securing the manor in total for the family began Tissington Hall around 1590. A stately structure with additions from later centuries, its long gallery dates from his lifetime (he died in 1619). This late Elizabethan and early Stuart, or Jacobean, period was an era when, in the aftermath of triumph over the Spanish Armada, England excelled in the building of manor houses which were not military fortifications, and Tissington Hall ranks as a notable example in Derbyshire where they are particularly abundant – a county where indeed the trend towards building beautiful mansions was already well in motion some time before.

Gateway to Tissington Hall

21a.   Chatsworth House and bridge, begun just before 'the year of English liberty', by the main instigator of the Glorious Revolution, William Cavendish, 4th Earl and 1st Duke of Devonshire.

21b.   Wirksworth market place.

22. Effigy in the Vernon Chapel, Bakewell church, of Dorothy Vernon (1545-84), the Elizabethan heiress whose reputedly romanti[c] runaway marriage brought Haddon to the Manners family, later Dukes of Rutland. Loc[al] histories often state that she inherited the ancestral home after 'The King of Peak', her father, died in 1567. But in fact he died on 31 August 1565 and Dorothy inherited early in [it] after her stepmother, Maud, had given up he[r] share of the Vernon estates in order to marry [her] love. The almshouse in Bakewell was founde[d by] Dorothy's husband, Sir John Manners, and t[he] Lady Manners School by her daughter-in-la[w] Grace.

23. Wingfield Manor: ruins of the banqueting hall and state apartments.

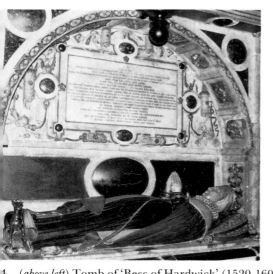

24. (*above left*) Tomb of 'Bess of Hardwick' (1520-1607), in Derby's Cathedral Church of All Saints, was erected by the lady herself several years before her death. It is situated in the Cavendish Chapel acquired by her second husband in 1557. At her feet is a stag, the symbol of the Cavendish family, on her head a coronet, denoting that she died as Dowager Countess of Shrewsbury. The lengthy Latin epitaph fittingly describes her as a magnificent builder.

25. (*above right*) Hardwick Old Hall: Bess's birthplace and ancestral home which she enlarged before her fourth period of widowhood, beginning in 1590, enabled her to build the New Hall nearby.

26. Hardwick New Hall, 'more glass than wall', Bess's masterpiece of late Elizabethan architecture.

27. Early 17th-century state apartments, Bolsover Castle, where Bess's Royalist grandson, the Earl of Newcastle, entertained Charles I in 1634, the entertainment including a masque called 'Love's Welcome', specially written by Ben Jonson.

28. Revolution House, Old Whittington, formerly the *Cock and Pynot Inn* where the seeds of the Glorious Revolution against James II were sown secretly in 1688.

IX From Haddon to Hardwick

In 1195 the future 'bad King John', in the absence of his brother
Richard I on crusade, granted royal licence 'to Richard de Vernon to
strengthen his house of Haddon, with a wall 12 feet high, without
crenaux', continuing somewhat prophetically, 'And I forbid lest anyone
. . . hereafter disturb him'. Nor did anyone ever try to attack or besiege
this, the most ancient of Derbyshire's great manor houses, in its romantic
wooded setting on the east bank of the Wye. Crenaux were loopholes in
defensive walls through which, for instance, arrows could be fired
at would-be assailants. But at Haddon, the worst fate awaiting any
unsociable visitor, unbidden or not, was said to be that, during magnificent feasts in its medieval banqueting hall, he might be fixed to the
wrist manacle on the wooden screen beneath the minstrels' gallery and
the ale or wine he should have drunk then poured instead inside his
sleeve!

Haddon Hall

Successive Lords of Haddon were noted for keeping 'open house' and
extending lavish hospitality. Household accounts preserve something of
the atmosphere of revelry as, for example, at Christmas 1564 under Sir
George Vernon, dubbed the 'King of the Peak' for his semi-regal lifestyle:
the Earl of Worcester's minstrels were paid a sum of 13s. 4d., the Vernon
tenants of Baslow the same amount for the carriage of a tun of wine, two
does were brought all the way from the family manor in Shropshire and
drinking jugs from Derby. Besides the usual festive foods of the time
such as turkey, capon, goose, beef, mutton, pork, cheese, apples and
nuts, other items for the table were oysters, eels, pikes and 18 blackbirds.
The wines included malmsey and muscadel, and a further sum of 11s.
4d. was paid for a gown for the 'lord of Christmas'.

The splendid dwellings in which such proceedings could take place
were at once their backdrop and centrepiece. Although Derbyshire is
poor in monastic remains, its richness in historic houses of architectural
styles and embellishments as manifestly different as some of their
colourful owners in bygone days is amongst its major attractions, the
best-known at Haddon, Chatsworth and Hardwick being for many
people almost synonymous with the county itself. Their great profusion
started to gather momentum amid Tudor economic prosperity, especially
after the Dissolution when the redistribution of former monastic property,
including lucrative wool-trade interests, augmented the incomes of some
leading local families and enabled them to enlarge and adorn or else

65

Carving of Sir George Vernon's initials, Haddon Hall

replace older structures. But the process had really begun in the later Middle Ages. From Edward IV's reign (1461-83), Crown duties from lead-mining had been let on lease to other holders and one family to benefit were the Vernons, whose lands had been steadily increased through advantageous marriages. Their 30 lordships in Derbyshire alone included manors such as Monyash and Youlgreave, where the tenantry depended on a livelihood of mining and farming combined. The Vernons remained Catholic at heart after the Reformation, but family documents imply acquisition of old abbey land in referring, for instance, to their manor and grange at Monyash.

Haddon's fascination is enhanced by its historic continuity from the Norman Conquest. At first a Peveril manor until this family's disgrace in 1153, it was afterwards granted to their resident tenant there, William Avenel, and passed in 1170 to his Vernon son-in-law. Since then it has belonged to only two families, the Vernons and Manners, whose respective crests of a boar's head and a peacock are beautifully evident in interior plasterwork and carvings. Of the house mentioned in 1195, some parts of the Peveril Tower (also called King John's Tower) still remain. Norman features also survive in the chapel, which once served the village of Nether Haddon, believed to have been depopulated when the Vernons received licence c.1330 to create their own enclosed private hunting park around Haddon Hall. Following this, the limestone walls and turrets of their home gradually coalesced to form the delight so often cited as England's finest medieval manor.

Its two-storied buildings developed around two courtyards, the lower incorporating the much-enlarged chapel, the Nether gatehouse and quarters for household servants and officials, while adjoining the upper were family and guest apartments, and from the 16th century, a setting for leisurely indoor walks or dancing – the long gallery, overlooking the south-facing terraced gardens above the Wye. To the 14th century belong the central range of rooms: the banqueting hall separated by its panelled wooden screen from the kitchen, buttery and pantry. This layout typifies the prevalent arrangement of its period, when the screen, divided by two entrances, was placed at the far end of the hall from the high table and dais partly to minimise draughts from outer doors. The room behind the dais at Haddon, originally a cellar with great chamber above, was transformed in Tudor times to a private dining-room. If the Haddon estates could provide limestone, lead and oak for the mansion's structure, the household accounts show that they also helped to meet daily food requirements for its people, even to the extent that the mid-16th century hermit on Vernon land at Harthill Moor supplied rabbits. Yet the family enjoyed rare delicacies too – such as melons long before these were easily obtainable in England.

High offices for Haddon's medieval knights included a Speaker of the House of Commons and a Knight Constable of England, but the family prestige grew markedly when Sir Henry Vernon became Governor and

Treasurer to the first Tudor Prince of Wales. The young Prince Arthur's last visit to Haddon in 1501 was traditionally portentous, in that a dream he had foretelling his forthcoming marriage and death came true within a few months. In 1517, well into his younger brother Henry VIII's reign, the Vernons were at the centre of a rift between the King and the great Cardinal Wolsey, each of whom wished the newly-widowed Lady of Haddon to marry a favourite of his choosing. Honours were even when Henry offered Wolsey the wardship of her three-year-old son, the future Sir George, which was refused, but the King emerged the eventual victor – as he did too in their rift concerning his own marriage 10 years later, which presaged the English Reformation.

The third marriage of Sir George's mother linked the Vernons with the Manners family. But the union which brought Haddon to the latter after almost 400 years of Vernon rule came two generations later. Sir George himself had no male heir, but two daughters: Margaret, born in 1540, and Dorothy in 1545. The Haddon accounts detail his £6 in travelling expenses in September 1555 to negotiate 'the marriage be-twyxt' Margaret and Sir Thomas Stanley, the Earl of Derby's second son, which took place early in 1558. In that year too his first wife died and a young Derbyshire gentlewoman, Maud Longford, was forced by her family to marry 'age far spent' (he was 44!). Beyond this, a six-year gap in the accounts throws no light on whether Dorothy's marriage to John Manners, the Earl of Rutland's younger brother, was arranged in the customary way.

The story of their elopement from Haddon due to her father's disapproval, so often dismissed for lack of direct documentary evidence, at the very least takes account of their two families' differences in religious leaning in early Elizabethan times. The 'King of the Peak' was certainly a formidable man, who had once had a servant of his hanged for murder, without a legal trial. While the usual version that Dorothy's romantic escapade occurred on the night of Margaret's wedding around 1563 does not accord with the few known facts; the first published account of it, which gave the setting as a great hunting festival that year, seems more possible. The author, Allan Cunningham, appears clearly to have based his story on an oral tradition well-established round Haddon. The first document to mention Dorothy *Manners* was her father's will made shortly before his death in August 1565. A near-contemporary rhymed chronicle on the Vernons gives sure hints of untoward events, disclosing that through Dorothy's marriage 'goodlie landes' passed out of the family name (she had several potential suitors amongst her Vernon cousins), 'For which great Talbott was ye more to blame'. This line has been described as 'puzzling' and 'great Talbott' suggested as Dorothy's uncle, Sir Gilbert Tailbois, who died some years before her birth. He was in fact none other than George Talbot, 6th Earl of Shrewsbury, the local 'power' then in Derbyshire – known as the 'Great Earl' – and John Manners' brother-in-law, besides his close and loyal friend, undoubt-

Garden terrace, Haddon

67

Oriel window in the banqueting hall, Wingfield Manor

edly a valuable ally if the young pair truly did find themselves at odds with Sir George. Ironically, the last Vernon left Haddon to his widow for her lifetime, but Maud soon also 'pleased herself' by marrying into a staunchly Protestant family, much to the dismay of her own. She revoked all her interests in Vernon property: from 1567, their Derbyshire lands, including Haddon belonged to Dorothy and John.

Although the Earls of Shrewsbury owned vast estates throughout the Midlands, a favourite residence was Wingfield Manor near the village of South Wingfield, which the 2nd Earl had bought in the 1450s from Ralph, Lord Cromwell, Treasurer of England. Begun in 1441, the house was completed by this Earl (Sir Henry Vernon's father-in-law) around 1458, and never subsequently much altered. Its position crowning a steep hill was defensively strong, and though there was accommodation for guards, the buildings at Wingfield very much reflected the emphasis on comfort and aesthetic adornment. Like Haddon, it was erected around two courtyards, had a high watch-tower and also a banqueting hall with traceried Gothic windows, the one lighting the dais a most unusual oriel of late Perpendicular. The hall, now roofless but still impressive in ruin, did not, as at Haddon, occupy the middle range – rather, together with the grand state apartments beyond its decorative 'screen' end, almost the whole north side of the mansion. To the left of these were the kitchen and other service rooms, and beneath, a magnificent pillared undercroft, presumed to have been a storehouse for food and wine.

The 4th Earl had hoped to entertain Henry VIII at this 'pore house' and hunt with him in Duffield Frith during a northern royal progress in 1541, but died here suddenly before the arrangements were finalised. Wingfield's most evocative historical links are with the 6th Earl and his tragic captive, Mary Queen of Scots, of whom fuller mention is made in Chapter XI.

Another of Mary's more congenial prisons was Chatsworth, the late Tudor version of which William Camden described succinctly as 'a house really large, neat and admirable . . . finished at great expense by Elizabeth, a most famous lady at present Countess of Shrewsbury'. The late 16th-century 'age of queens' was an era of ascendancy for women – the first since Saxon times – but few epitomised the spirit of that rising influence more than the Great Earl's second countess, better renowned as Bess of Hardwick. (Lady Gertrude Manners, his first wife, died in 1566.) Her life-story was that of the local girl who had not only 'arrived', but had done so with spectacular success. The daughter of John de Hardwick, she came of lesser country gentry but had a genius for marrying land-owners who left her rich estates. Her marriage to Shrewsbury, her fourth spouse, in 1568 was economically a merger between two great commercial enterprises with concerns in farming, shipping, lead, iron, coal and timber. That wealth's continuance within their families was partially ensured by the marriages of her eldest son to Shrewsbury's youngest daughter and his second son to her second daughter.

Entrance to the banqueting hall and state apartments, Wingfield

Derbyshire lands bequeathed by her youthful first husband, Robert Barlow, provided Bess with income from lead-mining. The substantial legacy of her second husband, Sir William Cavendish, including life interests in Chatsworth, Ashford and Buxton was, however, the crucial factor relating to the county's great houses, the future of Bess and her six surviving Cavendish children. Sir William had served Henry VIII as a commissioner during the Dissolution and thereby gained much property, especially in Suffolk. For Bess's sake he sold all this and acquired new estates mainly in her beloved native county from about 1549. Before he died in 1557, the Cavendishes began to replace a small manor house at Chatsworth with a five-storied mansion sited where the later 'Palace of the Peak', built by their noble descendants, now stands.

To her third husband, Sir William St Loe, Bess was 'my honest, sweet Chatsworth'. Honest she could be – often devastatingly frank – and at first to Shrewsbury she was 'swete one', but by 1584, 'my evil and wicked wife' and a 'burdensome charge' from whom he sorely wished to dissociate himself. Bess's own plain-spoken or written words suggest a character very near the well-known description of her as 'a woman of masculine understanding'. People who crossed her were 'false knaves' or 'right vermin' and, even in a fairly amicable letter to her steward at Chatsworth, she could warn, '. . . yf I lacke either good beer or good charcole or wode I wyll blame nobody so meche as I wyll do you . . .'. Bess's Hardwick accounts for 1599 record £40 being paid to her nephew, George Knyveton, when she dismissed him from serving in her household 'not in respect of his services but for his mother's sake'. Even so, she was one of the few women in Elizabethan England for whom its unique

Chatsworth House: an engraving from Bemrose's Guide to Derbyshire, *1873.*

Chatsworth Old Hall, built by Bess of Hardwick

monarch had a genuine liking.

What Camden rightly called the great expense of Chatsworth, where building costing around £80,000 took some 25 years, was a major source of discord between Shrewsbury and Bess. Another was the marriage, without his knowledge or their sovereign's consent, of Bess's daughter Elizabeth in 1574 to Charles Stuart, Earl of Lennox, who held a strong claim to the Tudor throne. The newly-weds both died young, leaving Bess with the guardianship of her royal granddaughter Arabella. When, also in the 1570s, she bought from her hard-up brother the manor of her birthplace, the Hardwick estate initially supplied timber for Chatsworth. The Earl, however, claimed the latter was his under their marriage contract and resultant legal battles, his unsuccessful take-over attempt by force and irretrievable marital breakdown caused Bess to concentrate on uncontested Hardwick.

Thorough, but speedy enlargement and alteration of her small ancestral home was required to complement her noble rank and prestigious position – so ambition allowed her to believe – as grandmother and guardian of England's next Queen. The now-ruinous Hardwick Old Hall, still with intricate plasterwork of forest scenes, engrossed her from about 1585-90 but was not yet complete when Shrewsbury's death gave her dominion once more over her own lands plus a prodigious widow's jointure. Within weeks the foundations of the grand, new 'Hardwick Hall, more glass than wall' (as local people called it) had been laid out about 100 yards from the old. Enormous windows through which daylight could stream and, at night, candlelight reflect in myriads of leaded panes, were fashionable splendours, together with exquisitely-crafted friezes, fireplaces and plasterwork ceilings, in the post-Armada era of confidence which found expression in the luxury of English manor houses. These influences are manifest in the long gallery at Haddon, but at Hardwick, built 1590-6 and so entirely within that period, they are all-pervading. Glass was plentiful in Tudor times and, since Derbyshire owners of great houses suffered no shortage of lead either, Bess, well into her sixties, could indulge in windows becoming progressively taller from the lowest storey housing the kitchen, hall and servants' quarters to the family apartments on the second, and long gallery and state apartments on the third. The six towers, each with her initials and coronet emblazoned against the skyline, add a fourth level of height to this H-plan mansion so sparing in its area of ground space compared with the earlier courtyard houses. Its architect is believed to have been Robert Smythson; its building material, like that of the Old Hall, was smooth-grained sandstone quarried on the Hardwick estate. For the marbled fireplaces so popular then, Bess also had a ready supply of raw material on her Ashford manor. Master craftsmen such as the marble-carver Thomas Accres, and plasterers Abraham Smith and John Ballergons (alias 'John Painter' in Bess's accounts) were employed by her extensively.

70

A tradition arose about a local prophecy which foretold that Bess would never die while she was building and that the severe winter of 1607-8 brought her schemes and thus her life to an end. True or not, she had over a decade to enjoy her resplendent new home, filled with its galaxy of tapestries, embroideries, period furniture and huge royal and family portraits. Elizabeth I's favourite, the Earl of Essex, is said to have been amongst its visitors. But her glittering hopes of a crown for Arabella came to naught, and intrigues surrounding the lady, thwarted marriage plans and attempts to abduct her from Hardwick marred Bess's final years amid her material wealth and power. Another granddaughter, however, became the Lady of Haddon when John Manners died in 1611 and the two younger Cavendish sons, William (for whom Bess built a mansion called Oldcotes near Hardwick) and Charles, their descendants and some of Sir Henry Vernon's were to keep alive her example through their close involvement in the erection of Derbyshire's later great houses.

Bess of Hardwick's monogram
surmounting a tower of
Hardwick Hall

X Education Tudor Style

During the process of educating his four children, John Manners of Haddon Hall sent his eldest son George to stay with his own brother, Roger, a member of Elizabeth I's household. As a result, the man famed for a reputed elopement in his youth and wild ride of some sixty miles from Haddon learnt this of his heir: 'he is a better galloper than you ever were and I am fittest to teach him. God keep him from falling, for that is all my fear'. Roger Manners, however, was anxious to 'doe something for George's advauncement' in Elizabethan society and reported to the boy's father in a different vein: 'you may write to him . . . to lerne to write better and to ryse earlyer in a mornyng. For two hours study in the morning is better than four in the afternowne'. Clearly, the more formal aspects of learning did not appeal to George, who often expressed a wish to travel! He was certainly no worse than many of his contemporaries, despite having a younger brother – another Roger – who was a 'living academic'. A royal tutor to Elizabeth herself, Roger Ascham, had noted regretfully, 'The young men of England go so unwillingly to school and run so fast to the stable'. With the sheer length of lessons in those days (beginning at 6 a.m. in summer months with subjects such as Latin grammar), perhaps that was only to be expected.

At Hardwick Hall, Lady Arabella Stuart also proved to be lesson-shy. As befitted her royal rank, her education was more academic than that of most girls in Tudor times. But the well-known instance when she took a six-day sojourn from studying while her grandmother Bess was away underlined the essential difference then between male and female education – that girls who received any schooling were taught at home. Alphabetical tablets called horn-books, which also included the Lord's Prayer, were the chief elementary aid to learning for both sexes and often made of wood, though some known Derbyshire examples, being of needlework, were reminders of the emphasis on domestic skills in girls' upbringing.

Boys over seven years old, rich and even many poor, were catered for increasingly by endowed grammar schools in post-Reformation Derbyshire, the most famous of which is Repton. In the mid-Tudor void left behind by the Dissolution, the earlier foundations were attempts by local Catholics to influence the emerging new society. No longer could wealthy men and women benefit their souls by endowing religious

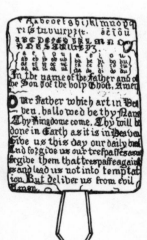

A horn-book

72

houses, but channelling money and property towards the upkeep of almshouses for the poor and free grammar schools provided another option. As monks and nuns had once prayed for their benefactors' souls, so schoolmasters and 'scollers' could now do instead. Both Sir John Port at Repton (1557) and Bishop Pursglove at Tideswell (1560) directed that prayers should be said at the start and end of each school day.

A victim of the Dissolution had been the Derby School attached to Darley Abbey. In 1554 it was refounded under a charter of the Catholic Queen Mary Tudor, which made the Derby burgesses its governors and granted former possessions of the suppressed abbey for its support. One of its recorded Cambridge undergraduates in the 1590s was John Cotton, the son of a Derby lawyer, who became vicar first of Boston, Lincolnshire, and then of Boston, U.S.A., said to have acquired its name in his honour. Schools at Chesterfield and Melbourne which had been linked to medieval chantry chapels had also ceased existence at the Reformation, but the former was re-endowed with rents and profits from Sir Godfrey Foljambe's lands at Ashover, under his will of 1594. When an Eliza-bethan charter granted the medieval borough of Chesterfield a mayor four years later, the school was established under the Corporation's authority on the site of the old St Helen's Chantry. Elizabeth's reign (1558-1603) was undoubtedly the 'take-off' period for Derbyshire's gram-mar schools for, besides Chesterfield and Tideswell, others were founded at Duffield (1565), Dronfield (1579), Wirksworth (1584), Ashbourne (1585), Staveley (1586) and Risley (1593). Although Repton had been provided for by Sir John Port's will in Queen Mary's time, that too actually became operational in her sister's.

Brass of Bishop Purs-glove, Tideswell church

Port had wished his school to be sited either in his own lordship of Etwall, where he provided also for almshouses to be built, or at Repton with which his connection was more tenuous. Here, the lay manor – the portion retained by the Countess of Chester after founding the medieval priory – had descended to his executor kinsman, Sir Richard Harpur. He bestowed Port estates in Lancashire for the school's maintenance, stipulating an annual salary of £20 for a 'well-lerned' graduate priest as its master of scholar and £10 for an assistant master, or usher. For its building, seven years' revenue from his Peakland property of Musden Grange was allowed. In the event, however, his wishes became reality after only two years, for a suitably adaptable building still stood within the ruins of Repton Priory and so, as at Derby and later Chesterfield, arose another example of a post-Reformation school associated with a pre-Reformation religious establishment. By a deed of sale dated 12 June 1559, this building – the former infirmary – was procured for £37 10s. from the priory owner, Gilbert Thacker.

Repton's first master is believed to have been Thomas Wightman, an Oxford graduate. Its first two undergraduates were admitted to Caius College, Cambridge, however, in 1568-9: the fact that one was from Staffordshire and the other from Warwickshire indicates its early evol-

Tudor-style doorway, Repton School

ution as a boarding school with a high academic reputation. By 1596, an observer could note that historic Repton 'hath lyttle left to glory on . . . only it famouse is by reason of a free school founded by Sir John Port . . .'.

The Derbyshire schools were in broad agreement that their aim was to teach grammar, literature and other good or godly learning. In keeping with this purpose was the donation of theological and classical books by Robert Pursglove to his foundation in his native Tideswell, while the very precise statutes he laid down for its smooth running give us an insight into the strict working regime of Tudor school life. The hours of study were 6-11 a.m. and 1-6 p.m. in summer, and 7 a.m.-4.30 p.m. in winter, six days a week, with short holidays around Christmas, Easter and Whitsun. Boys in the top two forms were permitted to speak only Latin during school hours, except when they were teaching younger boys, under the master's supervision. Pursglove dedicated his 'gramer schoole' to the Child Jesus, organising it along the lines of his own boyhood school of St Paul's in London, from where his career had eventually developed into appointments as the last prior of Gisborough, North Yorkshire, and Suffragan Bishop of Hull. Under Mary Tudor, he had reverted to the Catholic faith of his early life and, although continuance in this after Elizabeth's accession cost him his bishopric and other preferments, he remained of widespread 'estimation'.

The schoolmaster of Tideswell was expected to be like its founder: 'learned, honest, discreet and sober in behaviour . . . being a priest' or a single layman who, if he had the audacity to marry, would be 'utterly put from the said office for ever'. A new master had to swear an oath of fidelity to the school, pupils and property before formally receiving the schoolhouse key. Together with the vicar and churchwardens, he was also responsible for administering its endowed lands in Tideswell, Backwell, Taddington and Wheston, a quarter of their income being given to the parochial poor. Disciplinary warnings could be issued against him for offences such as negligence.

The seal devised for the 'Free Grammar School of Queen Elizabeth' at Ashbourne aptly included a master in cap and gown teaching two boys, whilst his assistant taught two others. Well illustrating the period also was its depiction of the enthroned queen with several petitioners, one of them holding a purse probably symbolising the school's endowments raised from local subscribers and 'divers well disposed' Londoners who originally came from around Ashbourne. Under its charter, the founding subscribers had the right during their lifetime to determine the appointment of the master, who was required to be an Oxbridge M.A. The chief subscribers hailed from the area's leading families such as the Cockaynes, Hurtes and Alsops, whose names were well represented amongst its governors. Subscriptions appear to have been paid quarterly, and the school's minute books detail items such as £6 10s. received from four Londoners in February 1603 and, a month later, 10 shillings from

Ashbourne Grammar School

74

Sir John Harpur, whose father had been so closely concerned with establishing Repton.

Apart from Duffield, the remaining Tudor schools resulted from individual wills: that of Henry Fanshawe in relation to Dronfield, Anthony Gell at Wirksworth, Francis Rhodes at Staveley and Catherine Willoughby at Risley. Besides the last-named lady, two other wealthy widows – Agnes Fearne of Wirksworth and Margaret Frecheville of Staveley – also left endowments to the schools of their respective places. Their example continued into Stuart times, ironically forging a link with the reluctant scholar, George Manners, when, in 1636, his widow Grace founded the Lady Manners School at Bakewell, endowing it with land at Elton.

Historical irony had the guise of tragedy, however, regarding the all-male Tudor concern at Tideswell School, when a master appointed by Bishop Pursglove himself in the 1570s, Nicholas Garlick, fulfilled in the 1580s the words on his patron's tomb that 'death to me is gaine'. Fitting well the founder's ideal for the schoolmaster, this man from Glossop would perhaps have embraced the monastic life, had the times still allowed. As it was, religious persecution had followed the Reformation and, as we have seen, its oppressive shadow touched even upon a dignatory of Pursglove's renown. Around the time the eminent old bishop died in 1579, Derbyshire people could be justified in counting the bitterness of local persecution high. Unfortunately, for some, worse was yet to come.

XI The Deep Divide

Padley Chapel

Early July in the Dark Peak sees the annual celebration of two Derbyshire customs only a few days apart, but which, in terms of the deep religious rift between Catholics and Protestants for over two centuries after the Reformation, concern beliefs at opposite ends of the Christian spectrum. On the Thursday nearest the 12th, pilgrimage and Mass at Padley chapel, near Hathersage, commemorate two Roman Catholic priests – Robert Ludlam and Tideswell's former schoolmaster, Nicholas Garlick – who, as a result of treachery, were discovered in hiding there on that day in 1588, from where they were taken to a brutal martyrdom in Derby. In the bleak Alport valley 12 miles north-west of Padley, a remote barn, where in Stuart times Nonconformist Protestant clergy ejected from their livings worshipped secretly and illegally together, is nowadays the venue of a commemorative service called the Alport Castles Love Feast on the first Sunday in July. 'Liberality of conscience,' so Derby's 18th-century historian William Hutton noted wryly, 'leads to gentle conduct; a strenuous faith leads towards ferocity.'

Hutton dated the spirit of local religious intolerance back as early as the 12th century when the borough of Derby paid for a charter giving its inhabitants the right to expel all Jews from the town. As a small child, he had been stirred with such sympathy by the tragic story of Derby's young Protestant martyr, Joan Waste, burnt at the stake in 1556, that he visited her place of suffering at the Windmill Pit, near the Burton Road. With an infant's vivid imagination he thought he had discovered there charred faggot remains from her execution fire, even though 170 years had elapsed since the actual event. Joan's horrific ordeal had been preceded by a denunciation of her beliefs, during which her physical disability of blindness from birth was made cruelly synonymous with 'blindness in the eyes of her soul'. Her fate aroused pity even in her own harsh times and was amongst the worst persecutions of 'Bloody Mary' Tudor's reign. During this, however, when Catholicism was briefly restored as England's official religion, a Protestant reformer called Thomas Becon found safe refuge with the Alsop family at Alsopen-le-Dale, near Ashbourne. His writings, while praising his hosts, inveighed against the general Peakland fervour for hearing Mass and matins, 'superstitious worshipping of saints', 'pattering' upon rosary beads and 'other popish pedlary'.

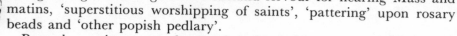

But other written records revealed clearly that the local strength of

Mary Queen of Scots

the Roman faith was not confined to the Peak. In a religious census of 1677 its adherents formed the highest proportion in England in relation to the total population, despite more than a century of tribulation. Almost a quarter of Hathersage's villagers then aged over sixteen, for example, were Catholics – 140 compared with 440 Anglicans, but lowland Norbury, south-west of Ashbourne, had a near-equal split of 65 and 74; at West Hallam in east Derbyshire, the respective numbers were 40 Catholics and 107 Anglicans. The bitter maelstrom that was the legacy of doctrinal differences was exacerbated both by national and local events, some directly entangling this divided county's history with the extraordinary ill-fortune which troubled the royal House of Stuart through several generations, from Mary Queen of Scots to her great-great-great-grandson Bonnie Prince Charlie.

Today we can only imagine the sensation caused by Mary's first arrival, at the start of her long captivity, in an area where so many people shared her Catholic faith. The Elizabethan laws re-establishing Protestantism in 1559 had expressly allowed those who inclined towards 'papistry' to continue, provided they conformed outwardly to the Church of England by attending its services. While Catholics elsewhere readily complied, this was not so in Derbyshire and the name 'recusants' given to those staunch enough to defy the law came into frequent use. Heavy fines, loss of prestigious offices and even of liberty became their lot from c. 1560-1. As we have seen in earlier chapters, the county's Catholics included some of its leading residents: Bishop Pursglove and the Longford family, for example. To these were added the Gerards (descendants of Sir John Port), the Eyres, Fitzherberts of Norbury, Sacheverells of Morley, Powtrells of West Hallam, the Babingtons, Bassetts, Draycotts, Foljambes and Poles. Mary's presence in Derbyshire gave them new heart, for as she herself said, 'An evil conscience cannot rest in peace'.

She was just 26 when she was placed in the 6th Earl of Shrewsbury's custody in 1569. 'I know her to be a stranger, a papist, my enemy', he wrote, to counter complaints of his kindness towards her and tendency to show her off to his visitors. With such notable historical characters as the Earl, his wife Bess of Hardwick, his close friends John Manners and Dorothy Vernon of Haddon Hall, Mary enjoyed musical festivities at Wingfield Manor and Chatsworth. Her first spell of imprisonment at the latter in the summer of 1570, however, also brought sharply into focus her divisive effect on the local populace. The discovery of a rescue plot left Dorothy in the unenviable position of being close kin both to the Queen's jailer and the leading conspirator – her sister's husband, Sir Thomas Stanley. Her own husband's loyal support of Shrewsbury was a mainstay, though she herself faced conflicting sympathies. The plot had suitably conspiratorial ingredients: secret codes, secret messages, four cloak-and-dagger meetings at 5 a.m. on the high moors above Chatsworth and, sadly, betrayal by one George Rolleston. The chief participants included his father Francis, Sir Thomas Gerard of Etwall,

Queen Mary's Bower, Chatsworth: she reputedly took exercise in its rooftop garden

Brass of Queen Mary's servant John Beaton in Edensor church: the motto translates as 'At home and abroad'

John Hall (a former Shrewsbury servant) and John Beaton, master of Mary's household. Their rescue attempt remained but a dream, although it ensured that in future the Scottish Queen was more strictly guarded and all the plotters except Beaton, who had died of dysentery, were confined in the dreaded Tower. An indirect, though more ominous result of this failed intrigue concerned a nine-year-old Catholic pageboy called Anthony Babington serving then in Shrewsbury's household. He came from Dethick, near Wingfield Manor, and his own plot to release Mary 16 years later was her undoing.

The possibility that other escape plans might attract her supporters was ever-present when Mary took the waters at Buxton. Not only did she meet many noble guests at Shrewsbury's town house there, but her greater access to the outside world soon started rumours of her increasing popularity through her small acts of alms-giving to the poor and disabled. During Mary's 1584 visit, Elizabeth prohibited an assembly of Peak Forest freeholders three miles away, because they were 'backward . . . and ill affected in religion' – she may have quelled a potential show of support for her captive. Portraits of the two Queens aptly hang at different ends of the long gallery at Hardwick Hall, which is rich in mementoes of Mary, though she was never a prisoner there. Indeed, her opposition to Bess in the Shrewsburys' marital troubles robbed Mary of all contact with Arabella Stuart, her niece.

Historians have provided us with innumerable accounts of Babington's plot in 1586 and his, then Mary's, execution. But so often the fate of those left behind has been largely ignored. In his home county, at least the recusants attached no stigma to his young widow, who soon remarried. His daughter, named Mary after the captive queen, died when she was eight. The web of religious tension worsened dramatically between the Stanley and Babington plots after a 1570 papal bull excommunicated Elizabeth and declared her Catholic subjects free of allegiance to her. A recusant list of this period mentioned a carpenter and mason called Green, 'dwelling at Morley', who made all the secret 'hiding-holes' for concealing priests in local Catholics' houses during the ever-increasing searches made by the Protestant authorities. To the Catholic laity, English priests ordained of necessity in Catholic countries of Europe were missionaries who kept their faith alive despite adversity; to the Protestants, they were foreign spies and traitors, liable to the death penalty after a law of 1584, along with anyone who harboured them. A famous Jesuit priest was Etwall's John Gerard, son of Sir Thomas. His autobiography told graphically of the perils intrinsic to his work: travelling around the country in disguise, being cramped in hiding-holes for hours and days with little .food, being betrayed, imprisoned and tortured, and planning his escape with the aid of letters written secretly in orange juice to friends.

Even Shrewsbury, Derbyshire's Lord Lieutenant, admitted the usual futility of searches, but when fears of invasion by Catholic Spain reached fever-pitch in 1588 instructed his Deputy, John Manners, to keep strict surveillance over all known recusants in High Peak Hundred. The fateful 12 July when the 'Great Earl' himself raided Padley Hall was the very day when the Armada set sail. He went there to arrest John Fitzherbert, whose own son had divulged his father's whereabouts (this young man was later rewarded with confiscated Fitzherbert property). In achieving much more than its primary aim when the two priests, Ludlam and Garlick, were found in chimney hollows, the search began the worst trauma in the many religious sufferings associated with the Elizabethan Fitzherberts and their Stuart descendants. John Fitzherbert, who with his nine siblings had promised their dying father at the Dissolution that they would never acquire monastic land, was one of several who died in prison – but, as Padley chapel's windows now depict, the priests were hanged, drawn and quartered in Derby on 25 July, together with a third priest, Richard Sympson. It is a curious fact that Padley manor, which came to the Fitzherberts of Norbury when Sir Thomas married Anne Eyre, had passed to the latter staunchly Catholic family through a 15th-century marriage forbidden due to some Eyre ancestral 'dark deed' which had merited excommunication. This union, however, between Robert Eyre and Joan Padley had led to endowments for Hathersage church and the founding of Stoney Middleton church.

Brass effigies of Robert and Joan at Hathersage typify their period, but even more evocative of its turbulent era is the early Stuart brass of Rowland and Gertrude Eyre in Great Longstone church. Although they conformed outwardly, the couple are portrayed with rosaries, but the crucifix once engraved between them was hammered out, probably by Protestant extremists. Religious dissent raised a new spectre in the 17th century amongst Protestants themselves, adding in time a new dimension of repression. The differences between 'High Church' Anglicans and the more austere Puritans splintered them too along political lines: when the Civil War between king and parliament began in August 1642, Bess of Hardwick's grandson, the Earl of Newcastle (later the 'Loyal Duke'), who had earlier lavished £15,000 on entertaining Charles I at Bolsover Castle, took command of the northern Royalist army; Sir John Coke of Melbourne, however, whose Puritan leanings had brought his dismissal as Charles's principal Secretary of State, soon had to flee his Derbyshire home due to Royalist harassment. Even Thomas Hobbes, then a tutor at Chatsworth, who wrote in his famous philosophical work *Leviathan*, 'Seeing there are no signs nor fruits of religion but in man only, there is no cause to doubt but that the seed of religion is also only in man . . .', saw fit to escape abroad because he advocated a powerful monarchy.

From 13-16 September 1642, Charles was in Derby, appropriating weapons and borrowing money for his army, whose pillaging had already antagonised much of the East Midlands. South of the Trent, Derbyshire was often raided by Royalist garrisons at Ashby and Tutbury, and in the north, by Newcastle's troops. Derby itself was never attacked, but

Simulated stonework cannons decorating the state apartments of Bolsover Castle

79

from October formed the headquarters from where the local Roundhead leader, Sir John Gell of Hopton, kept the county under parliamentary control for most of the war. The existence of Royalist strongholds such as Bolsover, Chatsworth, Wingerworth Hall and Wingfield within his 'territory' led to numerous encounters, of which Gell's capture of the vital Trent crossing at Swarkestone Bridge in 1644 was the most fierce. Swarkestone Hall was then destroyed, though remarkably Tissington Hall remained intact after a nearby skirmish. Gell's greatest 'annoyance', however, was Wingfield Manor, taken only after his besieging army pounded it with 'four great pieces'.

The effects of four years of strife on the long-suffering populace can be clearly gleaned from a letter written by the rector of Ashover, Emmanuel Bourne, to his cousin in 1646. At the outset, he had blamed both sides and distrusted Gell, who previously as the King's Sheriff had tried to collect taxes 'as an highwayman collects his plunder', even impounding and starving to death cattle belonging to Sir John Stanhope of Elvaston. But early in the war, Newcastle's soldiers arrived in the Peak, living 'at free quarters' and causing 'great slaughter of pigs and sheep and fowles'. A detachment already 'drunken and madd' made for Ashover's *Crispin Inn* (so named by local men-at-arms who fought in the English victory at Agincourt on St Crispin's Day, 1415). As a plaque outside the inn records, its landlord Job Wall refused to serve the unruly Royalists, but was then ejected and self-service prevailed until his ale was all consumed or wasted. Afterwards they demanded £10 each from Bourne and two other gentlemen for the king's use and, when implored to take less, accused them of being Roundheads and enemies, whose houses would be burnt down unless they paid. Before long, real Roundheads en route from the Peak to Nottinghamshire passed through Ashover, demanding £20 from the rector and threatening to take his cattle in part payment if he refused. Then Newcastle's army came back in 1643 'like demons destroying all they came neare and left the poore to starve' – after this, many people including Bourne supported parliament, the output from lead-mining saving them from total ruin. Even so, the king sheltered at Chatsworth in 1645 and Royalist troops again 'left us to starve'. In 1646, however, the old rector saw his home, Eastwood Hall, destroyed by Roundheads to prevent it falling into the king's hands, his furniture damaged in its hasty removal, the stained glass windows in his church smashed and the old parish register burnt because, being in Latin, the Puritan soldiers believed it to be 'full of popery and treason'.

Although the charge of high treason levelled against Charles himself in 1648 concerned events well away from Derbyshire, a relatively small area of its north-west amply reflects the mid-17th century historical ebb and flow. At Chapel-en-le-Frith 1,500 Scottish prisoners, defeated fighting for his cause in the short-lived 'Second Civil War' which he incited, were crowded into the church for 16 days in September 1648.

29. The Buxton Crescent: begun in 1780 by the fifth Duke of Devonshire, its cost totalled £38,500. The architect, John Carr of York, had himself 'taken the waters' at this historic spa in 1775 and the Duke's head carpenter during construction of the Crescent was William Newton, the poet 'Minstrel of the Peak', who later owned Cressbrook cotton mill.

30. Haddon Hall: bridge over the river Wye, built in 1663.

31. (*left*) Bakewell parish church.

32. (*below*) Bakewell town centre.

33. (*right*) Ashbourne parish church.

34. (*below*) Eyam parish church.

35a.   Bakewell bridge, with the town and church in the background.

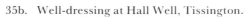

35b.   Well-dressing at Hall Well, Tissington.

Before their release, 44 died and more perished as they were marched away. First cousin to the family residing at Bradshaw Hall nearby was John Bradshaw, who as court president at Charles's trial sentenced him to death. Yet soon after the Stuart Restoration under Charles II, Peak Forest church was dedicated to 'Charles, King and Martyr', while the aptly-named village of Charlesworth was uniquely allowed to keep its Puritan minister after 46 others – including William Bagshawe, famed for his preaching as 'the Apostle of the Peak', had been removed from their Derbyshire parishes for dissenting from the 1662 Act of Uniformity. This reintroduced the more elaborate ceremony of pre-Civil War days to the Church of England services and forbade Dissenters, or Nonconformists, from gathering to hold the plainer, Puritan form of worship. But as in earlier times, law enforcement in Peak country presented especial difficulty. When Nonconformists assembled for clandestine services in the isolated setting at Alport Castles, lookouts could be placed on the hills around to warn of approaching search-parties.

One sect of Nonconformists had arisen, however, which even Puritans could not tolerate: the Society of Friends are said to have been named Quakers by a Derby judge when referring to the shaking and trembling of their founder, George Fox, during his impassioned haranguing of Protestant congregations. It was one such uninvited address, interrupting a church service in Derby, which earned him his first imprisonment in October 1650. The early Quakers gained notoriety not only for publicly and vigorously bearing witness to their faith, but for their belief in women's spiritual equality with men. In Derby too their first female preacher, Elizabeth Hooton, gave her first sermon during a service, for which she was imprisoned in 1651. Such treatment of the Quakers, begun in Derbyshire, continued throughout England until 1689 when, in the aftermath of the Glorious Revolution, a Toleration Act exempted all Nonconformists from religious persecution.

The pretty, thatched museum of Revolution House at Old Whittington, near Chesterfield, retains within its walls the nowadays blocked-up entrance to the 'Plotting Parlour' where the idea of the bloodless 1688 Revolution was hatched. The national events leading up to this united Protestant backlash which dethroned the Catholic James II were inevitably echoed locally after a fabricated 'Popish Plot' to murder Charles II in 1678 had brought renewed rigour to the imposition of penalties against recusants. The 'crime' of being a Catholic priest was still treasonous and, at West Hallam, Father George Busby was captured hiding between a ceiling and roof-tiles in the Powtrells' moated house after many painstaking searches by their Protestant neighbour from Locko, but unlike many priestly colleagues elsewhere in England he was reprieved from execution. Relaxation of the recusancy laws following James's accession to the throne in 1685 were soon clearly manifest in Derbyshire when Masses, for long said secretly in chapels such as those attached to Hassop and Wingerworth Halls, were celebrated openly. A

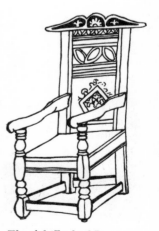

The 4th Earl of Devonshire's 'Plotting Chair'

81

Bonnie Prince Charlie

new Catholic chapel was built by the Eyres at North Lees, near Hathersage, and another restored at Newbold, close to Whittington. In the fateful Revolution year, these two were severely damaged by Protestant mobs.

Catholic influence had by then inflated so much that the county's Lord Lieutenant came from James's co-religionists, the Fitzherberts; after the Revolution, this passed to the chief conspirator in his downfall – William Cavendish, 4th Earl of Devonshire, who descended from Bess of Hardwick's second son. The unrecorded date of Devonshire's secret meeting at Whittington with two Yorkshire nobles, the Earl of Danby and John D'Arcy, was probably soon after the birth of James's legitimate male heir on 10 June 1688 altered the royal succession, until then belonging to his Protestant daughter Mary and her husband, William of Orange. Just over one hundred years before, Derbyshire's Anthony Babington had attempted to put a Catholic Mary Stuart on the throne and paid with his life; the successful attempt by another Derbyshire man on her Protestant namesake's behalf in 1688 shortly made him a duke. When William's invasion of England, invited by Devonshire and his fellow-plotters, finally materialised in November, however, the Earl's arrival in Derby complete with a supporting army and 'Declaration in Defence of the Protestant Religion' was coolly received, despite stirring news from London of James's flight into exile.

If the sad epilogue to Derbyshire's deep divide, the 1745 Rebellion, had also succeeded it would, as William Hutton observed, 'have borne another name'. James II's Catholic son and grandson, known in history respectively as the Old and the Young Pretender, reopened old wounds in Derbyshire through their campaigns to regain the Crown. But while rioting by supporters and opponents in Derby during the former's attempt in 1715 caused 'personal insults and broken windows', the physical presence of Bonnie Prince Charlie in the county from 3-6 December 1745 was like a throwback to bygone days. Protestants were truly apprehensive about the favour he might receive in an area with such strong Romish sympathies, Mass was once again heard in Derby's All Saints' church when he worshipped there and his advance guard pressed forward to their southernmost point at Swarkestone Bridge. Charles was proclaimed king in both Ashbourne and Derby but, if he expected supplies of men and money from local Catholics, contrary information reputedly imparted to him during lunch with the Pole family at Radbourne Hall en route between the two towns was a great disappointment.

Nor did the petty pilfering and intimidation perpetrated by his ill-equipped Scottish soldiers endear his cause here in the centre of English territory. Besides winter closing in, so were government troops. The momentous decision was therefore taken at Exeter House, where he stayed in Derby, for the rebels to retreat northwards via Ashbourne, the way they had come. The leaves had fallen and the landscape, bleak and wet with little hint of a future spring, was surely in keeping with the tragic Stuarts as the Prince rode away, severing at last their uncanny sequence of misfortunes linked with Derbyshire people and places.

All Saints' Church, now Derby Cathedral

XII Country Living in the 17th and 18th Centuries

Contrasts and curious anomalies featured particularly strongly in Derbyshire's rural life during the eventful Stuart and Georgian periods. In 1753, for example, an octogenarian bride was carried in her chair to the altar at Sheldon to wed a boy of fourteen. The well-known 17th-century angler, Charles Cotton, who described great rivers like the Danube as 'puddle water' compared with his beautiful Dove, agreed with Thomas Hobbes that Peak Cavern, Castleton, was one of seven wonders of the Peak – but, as the diarist Samuel Pepys recorded, to Charles II's courtiers it became the venue 'to send a man's wife when she vexes him' after the 2nd Earl of Chesterfield, jealous of his own lady's attractions, 'did presently pack' her home to his Derbyshire estates. And when rainfall flooded the cave, local people who dubbed it the 'Devil's Arse' – especially the ropemakers living and working inside its entrance – had reason to call the Peakshole Water issuing from it the river Styx. Hathersage parish registers mention payments being made for 'hedgehogs' killed by parishioners and brought to the church-wardens, a practice encouraged in several places due to the superstitious belief that these little creatures used up vital supplies of milk by sucking cows. At least some churchwardens had little excuse for suffering from insomnia, for the left eye of a hedgehog fried in linseed oil was apparently held to be a most effective remedy.

Young Derbyshire girls, however, may well have welcomed a bout of insomnia on St Valentine's Eve, when a unique county custom involved them running 12 times around the outside of their local church at midnight, sowing hempseed and chanting the following rhyme, in the hope of seeing their future husbands:

> I sow hempseed, hempseed I sow
> He who loves me best
> Come after me and mow.

Maiden's garland, Ashford-in-the-Water church

Fatalities caused by such exertions were not unknown, in which cases the more widespread ancient custom of maidens' garlands may have been occasioned. These tributes to the early and unmarried dead were wreaths of white paper flowers, lovingly made by friends and relatives and borne at the head of girls' funeral processions. Often pairs of gloves and 'sundry coloured ribbons in tokens of goodwill' adorned the garlands, which afterwards were hung up as memorials inside village churches. Derbyshire examples still survive at Trusley, Matlock and

Hunting tower,
Chatsworth

exploits of two girls: at Over Haddon in 1668, Martha Taylor lived through a year-long fast and in 1762, when the jilted maiden Hannah Baddaley leapt from Lovers' Leap at Stoney Middleton, her voluminous skirts billowed out, parachute-fashion, to save her.

It was at Over Haddon in the 16th century that the villagers had broken down hedges, put up around hitherto common land by the Abbot of Leicester, and grazed their cattle. Enclosures, the nationwide process entailing large areas of arable land and pastures for centuries held in common being hedged, fenced or walled in by landlords, often for sheep-grazing, caused great hardship to the English rural poor. In Derbyshire, it had begun in the Middle Ages but gathered momentum in the 17th and 18th centuries, producing visible changes in the landscape. Peakland visitors such as the writers Celia Fiennes and Philip Kinder remarked on the area's miles of dry-stone wall 'inclosures', so characteristically different from the hedged and fenced appearance of the lowlands. The medieval strips were perpetuated around upland villages by the 17th-century walls separating them into long, narrow fields. At Chelmorton, for example, they contrast markedly with the wider rectangles of the adjacent 18th-century enclosures. Records show that the earlier 'strip-shape' enclosures came about through private agreements between villagers, which – with the sanction of their manorial lord – consolidated arable holdings, a clear instance being at Ashford in 1608 when William Wright surrendered to William Monsal several half-acre strips lying between the latter's lands in exchange for several Monsal half-acre strips situated between his own.

But the many instances of confrontation flared up, almost inevitably, when enclosures affected common lands and wastes which were the only pastures the poorer inhabitants had. Such an occurrence caused riots even at Derby in 1603-4 over the loss of fields adjoining the Derwent in which the townsfolk had previously held common rights. 'How it will be good for the poor when the commons are taken away, I yet see not', lamented a kinsman of Sir John Coke's in a letter concerning Melbourne enclosures in 1632. Whatever Sir John's own views, the Earl of Huntingdon was 'fully resolved' to enclose his noble domains there and had 'the consent of the freeholders'. By then common lands usually were enclosed with their consent, each freeholder receiving a portion of land in compensation. During these turbulent times, such arrangements extended into the 1700s and so we find from contemporary documents that two pastures named Hollington and Green Moor at Tissington were enclosed in 1674, but Eyam Pasture was not divided by agreement of its freeholders into 'adequate and proportionable parts' of about six acres each until 1702. In 1726, Scarcliffe's enclosures were Derbyshire's first under a new Parliamentary award system which appointed three commissioners as surveyors and valuers of the land, and assessors of the various claims made to it. Again, documents reveal a far later date for similar acts, for example at Marston-on-Dove in 1789.

Long-protracted, and also a major legal result of enclosures,was the disafforestation of the two royal hunting forests. Duffield Frith lands at Belper, Chevin and Hulland were divided *c*, 1633, with the Crown retaining a third and the freeholders two-thirds, but the years of civil strife meant that this was not finally implemented until 1670, under Charles II. Similarly, the High Peak Forest was split into two halves in 1640 after the freeholders had petitioned Charles I to release them from the severe forest laws, customs and 'incommodiousness' of deer feeding on their crops and grass. The deer were destroyed, but disafforestation received ratification only in 1674. The freeholders' portions were not fully enclosed, which permitted the poor in these areas to continue using such land in common.

Despite the medieval forest laws being rescinded, other archaic penalties such as the stocks, pillory and whipping lingered on. The latter was a punishment 'according to the statute' for vagrancy, a problem which had increased its troublesome presence after the Dissolution when the poor dispossessed by enclosures could no longer seek alms at religious houses. It was a problem rigorously subdued in Derbyshire, as elsewhere, by returning vagrants to their home parishes after their flogging. Having dished out such treatment, the justices of Appletree Hundred reported in 1631 that 'there are now no wanderers in this hundred'. Laws passed in Tudor times had obliged the churchwardens and overseers in each parish to relieve the poor, classifying them into the able-bodied and impotent poor, such as the sick and aged, in addition to 'rogues and vagabonds'. In High Peak Hundred, the able-bodied were usually found work in lead-mining. Children within this category throughout the county were wherever possible 'bound prentice'. From 1724, parishes could lawfully set up workhouses, and records attest to a certain deterrent value at least for one such institution built at Dale Abbey in 1738 to serve nearby parishes, in which 'great numbers of lazy people' soon after were 'content to throw off the mask and maintain themselves'. No out-relief being available to the able-bodied, the poor rate fell by half. However, others amongst Derbyshire's 30 workhouses towards the century's close did provide out-relief – at Wirksworth, to 92 people, while its inmates numbered two dozen.

The more exalted world of the wealthy had important repercussions too in local life, adding to the county's quota of great houses 17th- and 18th- century gems at Sudbury, Bolsover, Kedleston, Calke, Melbourne and Chatsworth. Their continuing individuality of style is strikingly exemplified by the two earliest: the diamond-patterned brick mansion of Sudbury Hall, England's best preserved Stuart home, and the battlemented, sandstone spread of Bolsover Castle, complete with keep and famous riding-school, which replaced its ruined medieval predecessor on an eminence almost six hundred feet high. Lordship of the manor of Sudbury had passed to the Vernons through the 16th-century marriage of Ellen Montgomery to Sir John, youngest son of Sir Henry Vernon of

Diamond-patterned walls, Sudbury Hall

Haddon. But the hall itself, begun in 1613 by Mary Vernon, was finished after the Restoration of 1660. Its interior adornments of plasterwork, ceiling paintings and carvings accomplished by the craftsmanship of Christopher Wren's contemporaries such as Grinling Gibbons and Edward Pierce embody the spirit of Charles II's reign which so gladly cast off Puritan restraint. Work on refashioning Bolsover started with its 'Little Castle', a skilful representation of the medieval keep, also *c*.1613, when Sir Charles Cavendish purchased the manor from his Talbot stepbrother (and brother-in-law!), the 7th Earl of Shrewsbury. Within its Jacobean panelled rooms Sir Charles's son, the Earl of Newcastle, housed Charles I during his sumptuous stay here in 1634. The Earl had by then completed the state apartments and school for classical riding, an equestrian art-form not unlike dressage on which he wrote several books with some authority, having initiated its practice in England.

Metaphorically, Newcastle's Cavendish kin at Chatsworth, the Devonshires, could certainly claim to have backed the winning horse when the 4th Earl and 1st Duke prospered after his part in instigating the Glorious Revolution. In these two centuries when Derbyshire gentry attained titles including several earldoms, the loyal Newcastle and conspiratorial Devonshire were joined by the 9th Earl of Rutland in becoming dukes (the Rutland title had come to the Haddon branch of the Manners family in 1641). Since the Revolution was essentially an aristocratic enterprise, the nobility gained the balance of national power between the Crown and House of Commons, providing an equilibrium which the 17th century of civil conflicts had so lacked. From 1750-90, the Cavendishes alone provided one Prime Minister and six members of parliament. Small wonder that this Derbyshire family was at the forefront of local opposition to Bonnie Prince Charlie, whose '45 rising was the most serious threat to that political equilibrium.

Great houses and parks were improved to befit the new, titled dignity of their owners, although Chatsworth House being the principal Devonshire residence, and Belvoir Castle in Leicestershire that of the Rutlands, helped to preserve Hardwick and Haddon Halls in their 16th-century appearance. The task of replacing Tudor Chatsworth actually began under the architect William Talman in 1687, the year before the Revolution, but by its completion in 1707 it elegantly matched the ducal status. The remodelled setting of parkland and gardens around the palatial complex later involved the skills of 'Capability' Brown and Joseph Paxton, the appealing feature of James Paine's bridge over the Derwent being added to the aesthetic composition in 1762.

However, a feature clearly not in keeping with the auspicious new surroundings was the Chatsworth estate workers' medieval village of Edensor nearby, which the 6th Duke caused to be demolished and rebuilt between 1838 and 1842 at a respectful distance out of sight. Another Derbyshire example of this occurred at Kedleston, home of the Curzon family since the 12th century. James Paine is credited with building the

Kedleston Hall

Georgian north front of Kedleston Hall, but in 1760 was replaced by Robert Adam, who designed the main, south front and the interior. While Chatsworth is famed for its Painted Hall, with wall and ceiling paintings by leading 18th-century artists Laguerre and Verrio, Kedleston is equally so for Adam's awe-inspiring Marble Hall, which utilised local materials including pink veined alabaster for the fluted columns soaring 25 feet high all around the room.

Display interwoven with the pageantry of Derbyshire country customs was influenced especially by the Stuart era. Castleton's annual Garland Ceremony ostensibly marks the Restoration on Oak-apple Day – 29 May – when a mounted 'king' in period attire leads a village procession consisting of his 'lady', dancers, musicians and the sizeable bell-shaped garland, weighing about six stones, which is worn over his head and shoulders, then afterwards hoisted up to a central pinnacle on the oak-adorned church tower. The traditional connection between oak and Druidic worship, and the principal ceremonial role accorded to the garland king in green costume probably indicates, however, that, like the Tissington well-dressings highlighted in Chapter VIII, this custom in its present form was a 17th-century revival of a much more ancient practice. Its king has been equated with the personification of the 'Green Man' in pagan fertility rituals or, in medieval Maytime festivals, with Robin Hood. Other surviving customs undimmed by Puritan condemnation during and beyond the 1600s include Ashbourne's Shrovetide football and, at Tideswell and Wirksworth, the practice known in other hilly counties too as 'clipping the church' – 'clipping' here assuming its Old English meaning of 'embracing'. A human chain surrounds the church with joined hands, as once pagan Celtic communities are believed to have done around their own hallowed sites such as stone circles: as evidenced in previous chapters, Christian churches sometimes occupied pre-existing places of sanctity.

At Eyam, a small valley called Cucklet Delph was the setting for worship during the desolate months when plague struck the village from September 1665-October 1666 and is nowadays that of the annual commemoration service for the victims. The pestilence claimed 259 adults and 58 children from a population totalling only 350, but was prevented from spreading to the surrounding district by the villagers' voluntary isolation and endurance. The drama of their famous story which has inspired numerous poems, plays and novels is well revealed by the victims' cottages and graves, their names and dates of death entered in the parish register exhibited in the church, and village boundary marks, where food and other supplies were left in return for money soaked in vinegar (a practice widely believed then to protect the recipients from the disease). Of necessity, a common threat united component parts of society against it, irrespective of age, rank or wealth, and the roles of assorted heroes and heroines resonate through local history. The young rector William Mompesson and the ejected Puritan

Plague Cottage, Eyam, home of the first two victims in 1665

minister, Thomas Stanley, worked together in ministering to the laity; the 3rd Earl of Devonshire organised outside provisions for Eyam, remaining close by at Chatsworth all through the epidemic; Mompesson's wife stayed by choice to support him in his work until she died in the plague's greediest month of August 1666; in one week then, a mother buried her husband and six of her seven children, digging the graves for three on the same day.

A century later, the poetess Anna Seward recalled her childhood in Eyam, in particular – having had a sister who died young – 'the low beams with paper garlands hung' inside the church. Yet shortly after the close of the 18th century, other rural observers were regretting some decline in 'ancient usages', including the custom of maidens' garlands. Advancing industrialisation was bringing irrevocable changes to local people and places. Even so, the late 18th century still spawned some colourful characters, one of whom was the Repton headmaster, Dr Stevens, noted for his amorous escapades despite the Bishop of Lichfield being happy about his moral integrity when appointing him. He is said to have died after a stroke, triggered off by a raucous fit of laughter at the antics of a performing monkey in Repton High Street.

36. Calke Abbey: a priory of Augustinian canons is known to have existed at Calke before 1100.

37. Long Row, Belper.

38. Arkwright's Cromford Mill, suitably dark and grim in appearance as the pioneer of industrial mass production. When the factory system spread to other countries, a German village was even named 'Kromford'. Richard Arkwright, who was knighted in 1786, lived at Willersley Castle, overlooking his first cotton mill on the opposite bank of the Derwent.

39. Silk Mill gates, Derby: one of the county's many fine examples of the craftsmanship of Derby's early 18th-century ironsmith, Robert Bakewell.

40. The old Derby Silk Mill by the river Derwent – nowadays the Industrial Museum.

41. The Clock Warehouse, Shardlow, built in 1780 and now housing the Canal Museum. Its archway over an inlet of the Trent and Mersey Canal enabled goods to be transferred directly from the narrow boats into the warehouse.

42. Derby Arboretum: the first public park in England.

43. Friar Gate Bridge, Derby: cast-iron Victoriana, dating from 1878 when the Great Northern Railway's Derbyshire extension line was laid from Nottingham via Ilkeston to Derby's Friar Gate station, and eventually south-westwards to Eggington Junction. The line was closed in 1962.

44. (*left*) Crich Tramway Museum: opened in 1960, its collection of vintage trams includes examples from Europe, Africa and Australia, as well as many from various parts of Britain. The museum also gained the facade of Derby's Georgian Assembly Rooms after the rest of the building suffered fire damage in 1963.

45. (*above*) Magpie Mine, Sheldon, had a long but chequered history, having been opened, abandoned and reopened several times during the 18th, 19th and 20th centuries. Local tradition attributes its bad luck to a curse placed on it by the lead miners of nearby Redsoil Mine when three of their number died in 1833 in a dispute over the ownership of a rich vein of ore. Magpie Mine, now a field study centre, was last worked in 1953-8 and its surface remains are among the best preserved of British lead-mines.

46. Windy Knoll, near Castleton: an old Carboniferous limestone quarry. In the cave in the foreground the bones of many Ice Age animals such as reindeer, bison, wolves and bears were excavated in 1780 by William Boyd Dawkins, who also uncovered the Stone Age horse's head at Creswell Crags. Windy Knoll is now a National Trust property.

XIII   Georgian 'Treasure'

Having been quarried, mined or dug since ancient times, Derbyshire's natural wealth in building stone, coal, iron, clays, alabaster, marble, fluorspar and non-ferrous metals, chiefly lead, underwent significant increases in extraction during the 18th century. The skilled construction of dry-stone walls during Peakland field enclosures, for example, entailed greater demand for local limestone and gritstone. The latter found more elegant use too as part of England's urban Georgian heritage when the Buxton Crescent was built by the 5th Duke of Devonshire in the 1780s, its architect John Carr displaying influences of Robert Adam in the richly-decorated ceiling of the former ballroom which nowadays – still with chandeliers – houses the town library. American Independence wartime profits from the Duke's copper mine at Ecton, Staffordshire, allegedly financed the scheme, but the influx of wealthy visitors to the fashionable new spa surroundings generated further local capital, for instance in creating a select tourist market for expensive vases, urns and columns wrought from Derbyshire marbles and fluorspars, particularly Blue John.

Derbyshire iron-working also provided for creative expression through the celebrated craftsmanship of Derby's ironsmith, Robert Bakewell, whose surviving legacy within the county includes the 'Birdcage' arbour at Melbourne Hall. The digging of local clays culminated in the high international repute of Crown Derby china from this time. However, the intensified activity which transformed Georgian Derbyshire from a predominantly agricultural to an industrial county levied its own tolls by variously scarring the landscape from which the raw materials were taken and, sadly, the surest way for an unwary rambler today to find one of the many thousand old lead-mining shafts strewn across the White Peak is to fall down one.

More visible lead-mining remains include waste hillocks and old storage buildings known as coes. What Daniel Defoe noted as 'the search into the bowels of the earth' for lead when he visited Derbyshire in 1725 has become increasingly necessary since surface deposits had largely been exhausted by the late 17th century. With deeper mineshafts, in some cases over three hundred yards, reaching closer to the underground water table, problems of draining away floodwater increased too. Early methods of tackling these involved using hand-pumps or winching water up in buckets by horse gin, the noble equine working such a machine

Detail from a Crown Derby plate

89

Odin Sough, Castleton

treading round it in circles also to bring up ore and waste. A more adequate remedy added to lead-mining vernacular the important new term 'soughs' for the horizontal drainage tunnels constructed between mines and the nearest convenient river. A sough's surfacing point, where its ochre-coloured waters are discharged into the relevant natural flow, became called its 'tail'. The first sough was driven from Dovegang Mine, Cromford, to the river Derwent in 1631-2 by Cornelius Vermuyden, the Dutch engineer who drained eastern England's fenland, but several of Georgian date required distances of over two miles each at individual costs in excess of £20,000. The longest, Hillcar Sough, built 1766-87, had to pass beneath Stanton Moor to link the Duke of Rutland's Alport mines with the Derwent and was associated with one of the first recorded strikes when a working week of seven days was imposed to expedite construction.

Technological advance pioneered by the development of steam-power in the 18th-century Shropshire iron industry was a major factor in the dramatic expansion of Derbyshire lead production, for the steam-powered Newcomen pumping engine invented in 1711 proved both reliable and efficient in draining the mines. Yatestoop Mine, Winster, saw the first Derbyshire installation in 1717 and, after improvements to Newcomen engines later introduced by James Watt, Old Brightside Mine at Hassop Common earned the nickname 'Eldorado of the Peak' for yielding 20,000 tons of lead ore during 1779-88. Gregory Mine at Ashover, of which a near-contemporary memorandum states that lead output more than quadrupled in the short timespan 1762-7, used over three hundred tons of local coal to power its Newcomen engine during the 14 weeks preceding 28 September 1771 – an idea of how vastly this one industry stepped up coal demand and consumption. Around 1802, Richard Trevithick added further engine improvements, resulting in the highly-regarded Cornish engine. Derbyshire's largest example, 'Jumbo', was to form part of the late 19th- and early 20th- century success of Millclose lead-mine, Britain's most productive, which is detailed in Chapter XVII.

Coke-fired ore-hearths and cupola furnaces replaced the old method of smelting lead in hillside boles during the early 18th century. Amongst existing remains from the processing of ore are smeltworks such as Stone Edge, Ashover and circles with millstones, such as that outside Odin Mine, Castleton. Here the ore, known as 'booze' when first brought to the surface, was crushed prior to separation from waste material by washing and sieving – this latter operation going by the intriguing technical term, 'buddling'. Odin Mine itself produced about three ounces of silver per ton of lead ore. The occurrence of zinc ore in several lead localities appears to have attracted minimal attention until the Georgian era, but by the early 19th century some twenty-four lead-mines also yielded about one thousand tons of zinc annually, for use in brass.

*Crushing circle,
Odin Mine*

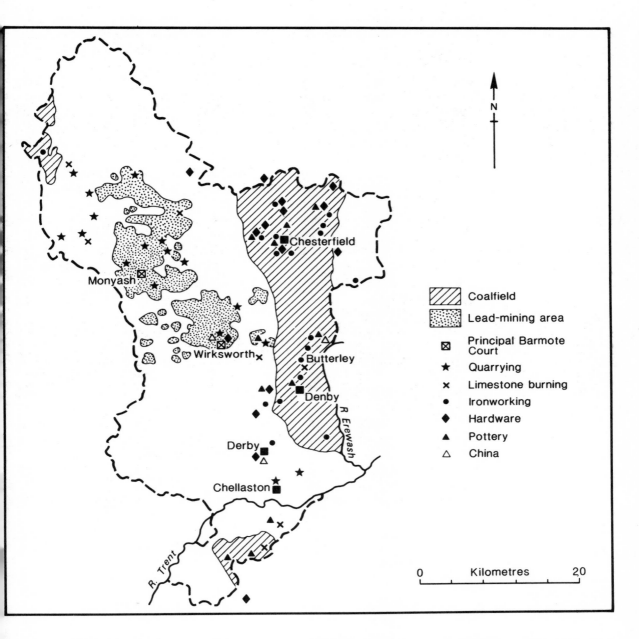

Map 9. Georgian extractive and related industries established a firm foundation for Derbyshire's rapid industrial rise.

The coal measures which have enhanced Derbyshire's economic importance in the industrial period form continuations of coalfields in adjacent counties – the south-eastern belt with Leicestershire, the small north-western with Lancashire and Cheshire, and the major, eastern area with Yorkshire and Nottinghamshire. Before 1700, coal fuelled industries such as brewing the 'excellent good ale' for which Derby was noted and limestone burning, the burnt lime being subsequently spread over agricultural lands or used as a flux in metal smelting. Many medieval and Tudor records refer to coal-mining, with its attendant slag-heaps and occasional accidental deaths. A dearth of wood had also increased domestic consumption. However, coal exploitation was so small-scale that Scarsdale Hundred, unintentionally an apt industrial name, long remained a favoured farming region, even being praised by Norbury's Sir Anthony Fitzherbert in his 16th-century *Boke of Husbandry* for its special practice of not loading 'donge, tyll harvest be done', which he believed was good for growing barley.

The county's natural woodland was so depleted by Georgian times· that coke produced from soft coal began to supersede charcoal in smelting iron ore at the same time as the lead industry's appetite for coal grew so rapidly and the pits themselves could benefit from the White Peak's improved mining techniques concerning drainage and sinking deeper shafts. Collieries opened by the Fletcher family at Butterley, Ripley, Pentrich and Heanor before 1717 had been added to by several in the Erewash valley before 1750 and output sales augmented five-fold. Both James Pilkington's *A View of Derbyshire* in 1789 and John Farey's mineral survey in 1811 attested to the burgeoning list of eastern mines, including places such as Ilkeston, West Hallam, Shipley, Denby, Smalley, Swanwick, South Normanton, Blackwell, Chesterfield and Eckington. Large numbers of young boys were employed in them until the mid-19th century, often starting aged five and, like the men, working up to sixteen hours a day.

The effect of 'cowkefied' coal on Derbyshire iron production was quantified as follows in Stephen Glover's county history of 1829:

	No. of blast furnaces	Tons of pig iron
Before coke was introduced	4 charcoal	800
1788	1 charcoal, 7 coke	4,500
1796	10 coke	7,650
1806	11 coke	10,000
1825	14 coke	19,100

Total output a decade after Glover reached 34,372 tons. The most important ironstone reserves were in the vicinities of Chesterfield, Staveley, Codnor Park and Morley Park near Ripley, and Somercotes near Alfreton. When the late 18th-century coke-fired furnaces still standing in Morley Park were 'in blast', their glow so illuminated the sky that it could be seen by their owner, Francis Hurt of Alderwasley Hall, several miles away. Benjamin Outram of Butterley Hall bought Codnor Park and established the famous Butterley Company there in 1790, consisting not only of furnaces, an iron foundry and steam-engine manufactory but limeworks, burning limestone quarried nearby at Crich. The foundry made iron bridges for diverse locations in the British Isles and India, war goods during the early 19th-century Napoleonic Wars, iron rails and water and gas pipes. Other important ironworks not surprisingly included Alfreton and a strong concentration in north-east Derbyshire around Chesterfield, Staveley and Dronfield. The iron industry also engendered an impressive variety of related hardware products: scythes at Norton; sickles at Eckington and Barlow; spurs at Bolsover; needles at Hathersage; steam engines at Derby and Chesterfield; nails at Belper, Chesterfield, Derby, Eckington and Wirksworth; chains at Duffield, Killamarsh, Measham, Dronfield and Unstone, these last two neighbouring places additionally making cutlery, along with Brampton and Derby.

Chellaston alabaster, or gypsum, which had once been much in demand for medieval altar-pieces and memorial effigies, but had fallen into post-Reformation disuse, was revived amid the Georgian industrial upsurge. Its estimated annual output was 800 tons *c.*1789 and 1,000 tons in the early 19th century. The highest quality stone, some of which was also quarried briefly at Elvaston, again found markets in artistic work such as monuments, and plaster was obtained from the crushed poorer quality for plaster of Paris, flooring and the pottery industry.

Products from Derbyshire's widespread potteries at this period ranged from earthenware jugs and posset pots to the celebrated Denby Ware and, last but hardly least, Crown Derby and Pinxton china, which have become collectors' items the world over. Brown earthenware was manufactured at Chesterfield, Brampton and Whittington well before 1700, but after this came also similar potteries at Alfreton, Belper, Church Gresley, Crich, Eckington and Woodville. A formerly flourishing industry at Ticknall went against the general 18th-century industrial trend by declining, however, because enclosures inhibited the potters' access to suitable clay deposits. The pottery at Denby was established in 1812 by the Bourne family, founders of the Belper works.

Derby porcelain was probably first crafted in the early 1750s, for which date a china-works near St Mary's bridge is mentioned in contemporary records. By 1756 its owner, a Derby banker called John Heath, was in partnership with Andrew Planché, a china maker, and William Duesbury, a china enameller. The reputation of its ornamental figures and tableware rose quickly and was regarded amongst the finest then produced in Europe. The Japanese-inspired Imari patterns so readily identified as Derby china, with their traditional colour combination of red, gold and cobalt or 'Derby blue', and still produced today, were

Eighteenth-century Crown Derby trademark

93

introduced around 1770. In the next few years, Duesbury became sole owner and royal patronage permitted the name 'Crown Derby' to be adopted, distinguished by the inclusion of a crown on its trademark. (*Royal* Crown Derby dates from 1890.) Duesbury's son steered the company from 1786-95, attracting to his employment a galaxy of truly gifted ceramic artists, some specialising in maritime scenes, others in landscapes, animals, birds and flowers. The best-known exponent of the latter was William Billingsley, whose realistic depictions of roses were particularly admired. One famous piece commissioned by nobility was the Kedleston Vase for Lord Scarsdale *c.* 1790, on which a tranquil view of Kedleston Hall and groups of Billingsley rose blooms appear.

The Duesburys and Crown Derby remained in tandem until the works were leased to Robert Bloor in 1811, whose eventual ownership lasted until the mid-19th century. Billingsley himself, however, left in 1796, taking with him several other employees from Derby to the newly-established Pinxton china-works. To him is credited the early, high quality of this short-lived enterprise and here he developed a pottery shape known as the 'granular body'. Pinxton's young owner, John Coke, was brother to the lord of the manor and had begun his interest in china when living briefly in Dresden. His business continued until 1818, but its production standards fell after Billingsley departed around 1802.

Derbyshire at the close of the Georgian era, in the 1830s, was one of Britain's leading producers of manufactured goods. But besides the extractive and related activities, there were two further elements in its industrial story which the next two chapters will consider in turn: water-power and vastly improved transport, in both of which lead-mining soughs had a direct role.

Pinxton china

XIV The First Factories

On a visit to a remote northern Pennine dale during the 1830s, Derby-shire's well-travelled author, William Howitt, found a factory standing in ruins because the local people had refused to work in it or subject their children to a 'daily incarceration' amid its heat and dust. Such an occurrence found no parallel in the river valleys of his native county, where despite strong adverse opinion the first fully-mechanised textile mills in the world were amongst the most notable wonders of the Peak for curious tourists on excursions from the spa towns of Matlock and Buxton. The magnitude of their enterprise, employing thousands of men, women and children both day and night, was unprecedented and began a social and economic revolution which went far beyond the banks of the Derwent and its rushing tributary, the Wye.

Cromford Mill

Because their machines were driven by water-power, the availability of its flow in sufficient quantity was more important in determining the sites of most early mills than the nearness of labour and raw materials. Industrial communities grew up around the mills, often in remote and rural surroundings. The greatest transformation from small, scattered units of production to the factory system came in the silk and cotton industries, while wool continued to be largely spun and woven by hand in the workers' homes, as it had since medieval times. A working day of at least twelve hours, six days a week, and the employment of very young children were characteristics of factory work until well into the 19th century, and their beginnings can be traced back as far as 1702, when the Derby silk mill was established by Thomas Cotchett on an island in the Derwent. The factory was considerably expanded by John Lombe in 1717, using machines based on models brought from Italy. By the 1730s it employed about three hundred people, one of whom was William Hutton, the later historian. His autobiography detailed graphically his youthful experiences during his seven-year apprentice-ship there. Rising at five o'clock each morning, even at the tender ages of seven and eight years old, he was expected to work until the evening. The discipline was harsh and a particularly severe beating from the overseer left him scarred for life.

In contrast to such abuses during its production, the spun silk itself was heavily protected in the 18th century, enjoying exclusive possession of the British market. Its chief customer was the Midland hosiery industry, which in Derbyshire predominated in the south and east. The

95

Richard Arkwright

making of stockings remained home-based until the mid-19th century, the stocking-frame machines being rented out to the knitters by master hosiers. The design of these machines had hardly changed since Tudor times, but around 1760 a sudden, major improvement took place when Jedediah Strutt of South Normanton perfected a ribbed stocking frame – 'the Derby Rib', as it became known, enabled closer-fitting stockings to be made and changed the face of the industry. To meet its increasing demand for silk, further mills, including one owned by Strutt, were set up in Derby. Great quantities of wool and cotton thread were also required, and in 1770 Strutt combined with Richard Arkwright to construct the first cotton mill at Cromford, some fourteen miles upstream.

They chose the site of a former corn mill where the Derwent's gritstone flow, augmented by the Bonsall Brook and Cromford Sough, could run Arkwright's newly-patented invention, the 'Spinning Frame', which consisted of two pairs of rollers, much speeding up the output of cotton yarn. 'Put in t'rollers o' t'spinning frame', he was later to instruct his portrait painter, Joseph Wright. 'It's them what made me t'brass'. His invention had initially caused him to move from his native Lancashire, however, for fear of its destruction by hostile cotton hand-spinners and his pioneering mill at Cromford aptly reflects this fear in its fortress-like appearance. Round, imposing towers guard the gated entrance and there are few windows until about fifteen feet above ground level. Not only was the factory built but also a village of workers' cottages, complete with church and inn. His workforce even sang of 'the Master', who literally owned the place, feeding and clothing them all 'from his bountiful store'.

Strutt started his own cotton empire at Belper in 1775-6 and in partnership with Arkwright set up more mills in the Peak at Bakewell, Cressbrook, Wirksworth and Ashbourne. Their factory at Milford was opened in 1780, the year before their business ties were ended, and he subsequently assumed control. (Arkwright, however, retained control of Cromford, and later became High Sheriff of the county.) The calico works Strutt established in Derby made the material wholly from cotton instead of the previous linen-cotton mixture – an innovation which in the face of fierce opposition from Lancashire eventually needed an Act of Parliament to deem it lawful. At Belper, James Pilkington reported in 1789 that 'every year, almost every month, new houses are rising up'. The workforce of 600 in that year expanded to 1,500 by 1815 and doubled again by 1833. Gun-ports were installed in the footbridge spanning the approach to the mill as a deterrent against possible attack.

A hosiery partnership between John Gardom of Bubnell and John Pares of Leicester resulted in the cotton mill erected at Calver in 1776, attracting a labour force of mainly women and children from the nearby lead-mining villages. In 1783, the patent for Arkwright's spinning machine expired, but despite this he built Masson Mill between Crom-

Gun-port, Belper Mill

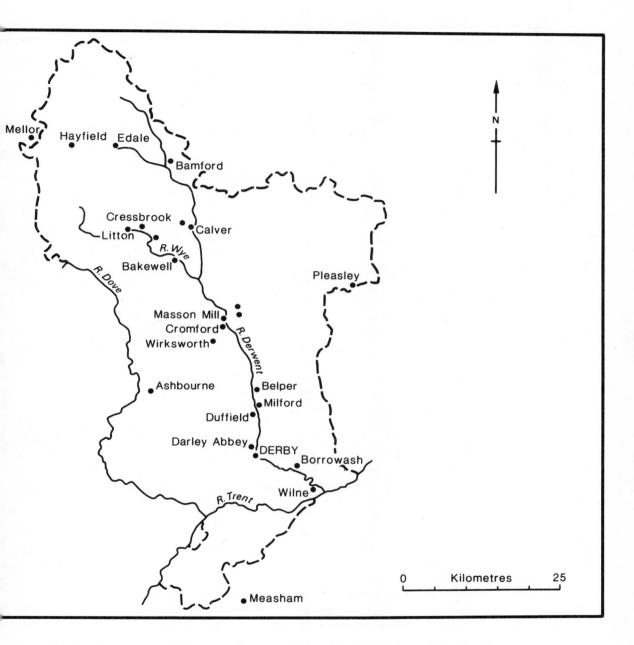

Map 10. Early water-powered cotton mills, concentrated mainly along the Derwent and its tributaries.

William Newton, the 'Minstrel of the Peak'

ford and Matlock, and encouraged the Evans family to extend their already substantial industrial interests in paper and metal to the development of a cotton mill at Darley Abbey. He was also associated with the spread of his invention to such isolated settings as Edale, Eyam, Little Longstone and Litton, in Miller's Dale. In 1790 at Mellor, then just inside the county's north-west boundary, Arkwright gave financial assistance to Samuel Oldknow to harness the power of the river Goyt. Oldknow, a former apprentice to his draper uncle, Thomas (who, with his own near kinsman Henry Hollins opened a cotton mill at Pleasley in 1784) became noted for manufacturing very fine cotton fabric.

The sight of the mills working at night by candlelight was described as 'romantic' by Dr. Erasmus Darwin (the grandfather of Charles), but that was a sentiment hardly shared by the poet, William Newton, the 'Minstrel of the Peak' who was 'confined to 14 hours each day of mechanical drudgery' during his life as a carpenter-mechanic for Strutt and Arkwright at Cressbrook. Only when the mill burnt down and all his tools were lost did his fortunes, paradoxically, begin to rise, for literary friends raised enough capital to obtain a partnership for him in the new mill occupying the site of the old. By the beginning of the 19th century, he was the outright owner and so, like the other industrial lords, in a position to direct the lives of his employees.

The authority of the factory owners, which was absolute during the long working hours, was maintained by patronage outside them. Some factory villages were so far-flung from major centres of population that the employers were virtually obliged to supply the basic necessities of milk, food and fuel for their workers. The importance attached to their welfare varied, for some employers were harder task-masters than others. However, nowhere was there a difference as sharp in so short a distance as that between Cressbrook and Litton Mills, separated by the beautiful Water-cum-Jolly Dale along the river Wye. Their remoteness meant that some of their workforce was comprised of pauper children brought into the area as apprentices, but whereas the two- to three-hundred under Newton's care were well-clothed, housed and fed, and given free time for recreation, the horrific tales emanating from Elias Needham's Little Mill told of cruelty in the extreme – of sadistic beatings, overwork and the children receiving so little food that they had to steal from pigs. William Newton took responsibility also for the spiritual well-being of his young charges, taking them to church and Sunday School at Tideswell each week and, if any of them had an aptitude for music, they were allowed working time for study. Newton's heartfelt opposition to child brutality placed him ahead of his time.

The Strutts too encouraged music and had a choir and orchestra recruited from their workers. Nor did they endorse corporal punishment, but instead had a system of fines imposed for offences such as: incompetence, idleness, absence from work without leave, theft, destruction of or damage to mill property, riotous behaviour at work and misconduct outside working hours. The Evans had a similar system, including fines for non-attendance at Sunday School. They used the money to finance a Darley Abbey medical service. Like the Strutts and Arkwrights, they also subsidised the cost of coal, meat and vegetables – but woe betide any male employee who did not doff his cap, or female who did not curtsey, when a member of the Evans family passed by through the village they had created!

Oldknow acquired so much land in the area around Mellor that his employees were totally dependent on him. He provided facilities for them to keep cattle and had his own herd to supply milk to them during work. The cost of all goods obtained from him was deducted from their wages, as was the rent for their houses. Unfortunately for the workers, his own desperate shortage of funds led him to operate a system of 'truck' so efficiently that he well-nigh eliminated all exchange of money between himself and them. His relationship with them has consequently been compared with that of a feudal lord.

A few Derbyshire hand-spinners continued to compete successfully with the mills, notably five sisters near Mellor who did so for almost fifty years. But factory organisation displaced them beyond the county due to Arkwright's determined expansion into Nottinghamshire, Staffordshire and even Lancashire. With the passage of time, water-powered mills too were destined to become an endangered species – and not only because of bouts of machine-breaking known as the Luddite Riots during the period of general unrest in the second decade of the 19th century. In the event, the hosiery industry suffered most from violence of this kind in Derbyshire, but when the Strutt family regaled their cotton mill workers with festivities said to have cost £10,000 to celebrate the end of the Napoleonic Wars in 1814, they were probably also glad that they had those gun-ports to help defend Belper and had formed a 'Milford Militia' to protect their property. National economic problems giving rise to a lack of work at the end of the war, and therefore hardship for the poorer classes, combined with the local problem of a cold, wet 1816, badly affecting both lowland and upland Derbyshire. In 1817 the parish register at Pentrich recorded: 'On the evening of 9 June an insurrection broke out in Pentrich, South Wingfield, Swanwich and Ripley, which was quell'd next day . . .'. A rising of poor stocking-frame knitters led by Jeremiah Brandreth aimed to capture the Butterley iron foundry, but failing that began to march towards Nottingham. They crossed the county boundary, to find that local troops were waiting for them and, although they dispersed, the ringleaders were captured and executed.

Exactly a century had passed between this event and the initial adoption of steam-power by Derbyshire's metal industries. The introduction of steam-power into textile industries towards the mid-19th century meant that mills were more conveniently sited in lowland areas in or close to large towns. The early mills in Derbyshire which came into this category were able to adapt and survive, as at Belper and Darley Abbey,

Cressbrook Mill

99

but in the more inaccessible places they went into decline. Nevertheless, in their heyday, there was no clear certainty whether Derbyshire or Lancashire would be more prominent in cotton manufacture. As the need for water-power lessened, the latter's more favourable position for the transportation of raw cotton through Liverpool came to the fore. Even then, its clay-lined canals which allowed the passage of goods inland were due to the genius of Derbyshire men and, when the waterway system was extended to reach the first factories in Derbyshire, communications began to open up in the county after centuries of difficulty.

XV   Changes of Carriage

When the national era of improvement in means of transport was in its early 18th-century infancy, a highwayman known as Black Harry who preyed upon Peakland packhorse trains was gibbeted at Wardlow Mires. In 1815, the gibbeting there of the murderer of the local tollgate keeper prompted William Newton of Cressbrook Mill to write the poem for which he is best remembered, urging the abolition of such punishment. The hundred years or so separating these two gruesome incidents witnessed the rapid development of Derbyshire's road, canal and tramway systems, the great material incentive being provided by industrial expansion requiring cheap and speedy conveyance of goods between producer and customer. A century further on, in 1915, World War I provoked a Zeppelin airship raid on Derby, by then long-established as a prime railway centre and already famed too for Rolls-Royce car and aero engines. Derbyshire's transport history, justifiably a fascination in itself with different generations of enthusiasts, has been intertwined with well-known names in many aspects of its progress. James Brindley, the 'father of canals', was born in the county, as was Thomas Cook, the initiator of package tours; George Stephenson, the 'father of railways', lived the last decade of his life at Chesterfield; to Benjamin Outram's name the derivation of 'tram' has been attributed and amongst the varied innovative works engineered by his Butterley partner, William Jessop, was the 4 ft. 8½ in. wheel gauge which became standard, both on national and international railways.

According to newspaper advertisements appearing in the *Derby Mercury* during the 1760s, flying machines were in existence well before the 20th century. The 18th-century versions, however, were horse-drawn passenger coaches, steel-sprung to ensure greater comfort (an innovation adopted only in 1754), which completed the journey from Manchester to London via Buxton and Derby in the relatively swift time for then of three days. They were superseded in mid-decade by post coaches, which took only two days. In the 1770s a major haulage company called Pickfords, originally formed in the Goyt valley, began operating 'fly-wagons' along this route which by 1813 had cut their original journey time of about four days to less than two. Although packhorse trains – locally called 'jags' – continued to carry goods in their panniers across remote Peakland areas until the 19th century, wheeled wagons and carts capable of holding larger amounts of produce were inevitably more

Newhaven Inn

suited to cope with escalating industrial output. The greater volume and speed of wheeled vehicles in Derbyshire was indeed a sign that its roads had been made more suited to cope with them, for until the concerted improvements throughout Georgian times with the turnpike era, English roads were rutted, unpaved and notoriously inadequate. But in highland Derbyshire, as of old, steep hills had further inhibited wheeled traffic. The mere handful of county roads deemed worthy of inclusion on Herman Moll's Derbyshire map of 1724 showed the Derby-Buxton route mostly following the line of the old Roman road, The Street. How different was the tangled network of intersecting turnpikes revealed linking settlements on a map in John Farley's *General View of the Agriculture of Derbyshire* in 1817, particularly on the eastern coalfield. Many present-day main roads are along the course of old turnpikes, for example the A52 from Derby to Ashbourne.

The basic principle of the turnpike system was to pass some of the costs of highway repair and maintenance from parishes to the growing amount of road traffic by exacting tolls. A law of 1555 had placed this financial burden totally on parishes concerning roads within their boundaries and obliged all parishioners to work six days a year on road upkeep. Turnpike Acts of Parliament, however, authorised local trusts to assume responsibility for legally-defined sections of road, along which tollgates could be set up for collecting toll revenue. Trustees were usually men of substance in whose direct interests improved communications often served — as the list of names illustrated, for instance, when an initially private Derwent valley road connecting Arkwright's mill at Cromford with Strutt's at Belper was turnpiked. Strutts, Arkwrights and the equally familiar-sounding names of Evans and Oldknow appeared prominently amongst the industrial grandees, the Dukes of Devonshire and Rutland amongst the local landowners. One tollgate on this road stood at a junction near the confluence of the Derwent and Amber, consequently acquiring the name Ambergate.

Statute labour on all roads stayed in force until 1835, though in practice parishioners could opt out by paying what was termed a money composition amounting to a small percentage of their annual income. A list of tolls is still preserved at Cavendish Bridge, Shardlow, where the London-Manchester road crossed the Trent into Derbyshire: the charge for coaches, chariots, landaus, chaise, wagons, wains and carts were between a shilling and half-a-crown, depending on whether the vehicle had two or four wheels; soldiers, cows and horned cattle could cross for a halfpenny each, but a penny was the toll for an ordinary pedestrian, as for any horse, mule or ass 'not drawing'. In 1738, this part of the road, leading on through Derby as far north as Brassington, was the subject of the county's first Turnpike Act. Others soon followed, one of which was the section of this long-distance route beyond Buxton, through Whaley Bridge. The intervening stretch over the firm, dry White Peak plateau demanded less regular repair. Early turnpikes aimed to improve existing routes, many of them ancient ways for packhorses, for which gradients such as 'Steep Turnpike', Matlock had presented little problem. Old guideposts ordered by laws of Queen Anne's reign (1702-14) can often be found beside Peakland byways, but the well-nigh impossible slopes for wheeled traffic caused some to be later abandoned as turnpikes, where more passable routes could be worked out. An alternative way from Derby to Buxton, via Ashbourne, was quickly favoured over the old struggle through Brassington and eventually turnpike trusts administered the entire length of the re-routed thoroughfare, a new turnpike being further created to replace the short stretch north of Ashbourne through Mapleton and Thorpe with the present route past Fenny Bentley and Tissington.

About halfway between Ashbourne and Buxton was the important meeting of turnpikes at Newhaven, where coaches connected also from Bakewell, Staffordshire and Nottingham, via Alfreton and Matlock. The Duke of Devonshire erected the present inn in 1795. Other well-known roads from turnpike days are Thomas Telford's highland link between Manchester and Sheffield over the Snake Pass and the also scenic Via Gellia, cut through its wooded valley originally so that lead from the Gell family's mines could reach the Cromford Canal, opened in 1793.

A warm flow of water from the Cromford Sough fed this canal, which was constructed by William Jessop and crossed the river Derwent by means of the Wigwell aqueduct, a method first devised by James Brindley. Canals had their Derbyshire debut with a branch of Brindley's greatest work, the Grand Trunk (later called the Trent and Mersey), finished in 1777. A native of Tunstead near Wormhill, Brindley concentrated for much of his career on developing, servicing and repairing water-powered and pumping machinery in mills and mines. The success of his first navigable inland waterway, the Bridgewater, carried by the long and novel aqueduct of his design over Lancashire's Irwell valley, brought in the canal-building era. The Grand Trunk followed his construction of the Manchester-Liverpool Canal. Its Derbyshire section extends from the Monks Bridge aqueduct over the Dove to the navigable Trent at Shardlow. He did not live to see the completion either of this or the other work he projected partially in his home county, the Chesterfield Canal, also fully opened in 1777. At Shardlow, however, many brick-built warehouses and cottages remain from the period when, thanks to his ingenuity, it became a thriving inland port (one of only two in England), where merchandise conveyed by road or in larger barges up the Trent was transferred to brightly-painted narrow boats — or vice versa.

Whether cotton, corn, cheese or coal formed the boatmen's cargo, tolls levied according to weight and distance transported enabled canal companies to recoup construction and maintenance costs. By far the main commodity was coal, so vital to industry yet so bulky too that the

Fanlight window - a frequent feature on Shardlow's canal warehouses

previous inefficient ways of moving it in areas away from navigable rivers had rendered its price high. Such considerations had understandably featured uppermost amongst coal owners and consumers alike when, for example, turnpikes set up between the Erewash valley coalfield and its Nottingham market during 1740-65 provided better access. But more distant markets were beckoning too in the southern Midland counties, emphasising even more the need for reducing carriage costs. The fruits of Brindley's work was certainly timely for the Erewash colliery masters (his first two canals had quickly lowered the price of Lancashire coal by about half in the 1760s) and from 1779, their own canal consolidated the promise of greater sales. Stephen Glover stated that the Erewash Canal engineer was Jessop – the construction itself was supervised by John Varley who had been Clerk of Works on the Chesterfield Canal. Starting at Langley Bridge, it winds mostly along Derbyshire's side of the Erewash valley to meet the Trent near Sawley, from where the Soar Navigation extended waterway links southwards.

A shortage of coal supplies in the opposite direction, from Yorkshire to the lower Trent valley, was instrumental in the appearance of further canals on the Erewash coalfield in the 1790s. The two in Derbyshire were the Cromford Canal, already mentioned, running from near Arkwright's mill to the Erewash at Langley Bridge, then on to Pinxton, and the Derby Canal, dating from 1796. Both Outram and Jessop, the next generation of canal-builders after Brindley, were concerned with its construction from the Trent and Mersey Canal near Swarkestone Bridge to Derby and then eastwards to the Erewash at Sandiacre, an additional branch extending from Derby to Little Eaton. Outram also engineered the small Nutbrook Canal (1795), from Shipley colliery to the Erewash near Trowell, and Peak Forest Canal (1797) from Whaley Bridge into Cheshire and Lancashire. Another small canal from this busy decade was the Adelphi (1799), joined to the Chesterfield Canal for carrying goods from Duckmanton's ironworks to Staveley.

More usually, tramways united mines, works and quarries with canals. The first sight of horses pulling wagons along flanged iron rails probably occurred in Shropshire c.1767, but not above ground in Derbyshire until 1788, at Wingerworth, having previously been adopted in coal mines. Again, however, the work of Outram and Jessop contributed significantly to developing an inexpensive mode of transport. Another early track, the Outram Way, connected Denby to the Derby Canal at Little Eaton. In addition to its rails, the Butterley Ironworks also cast iron rims for the wagon wheels. The two men differed in their views regarding whether the flange, or projecting rib for keeping truck on track, should be positioned on the wheels or rails. Jessop favoured a flanged wheel on a flat rail and produced his distinctive 'fish-bellied' rails of cast iron which, like his 4 ft. 8½ in. standard wheel gauge, later became devices in George Stephenson's work, but using wrought iron. Nowadays the Tramway Museum at Crich runs its vintage trams on a

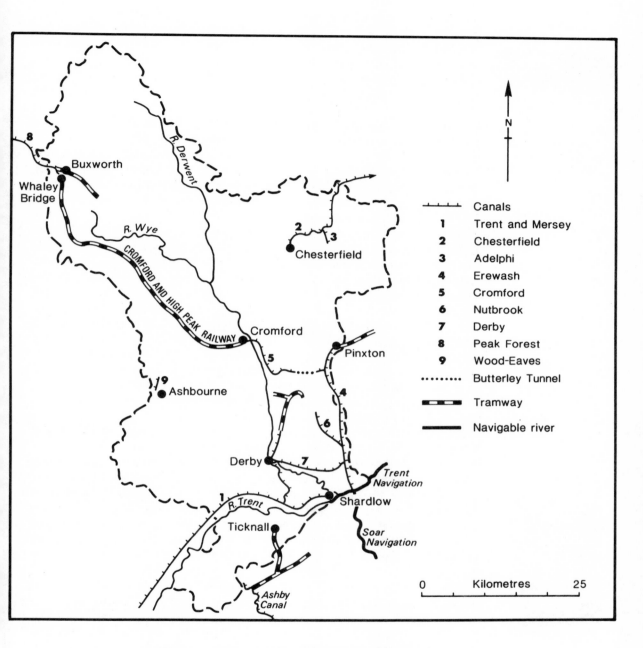

Map 11. Canals, longer tramways and river navigation.

rebuilt section on a Stephenson narrow gauge line which linked Cliff Quarry with limekilns and the Cromford Canal at nearby Ambergate.

Most Derbyshire tramways were laid over short distances, but there were notable local exceptions. Outram numbered amongst the many he constructed the lines from Ticknall limeworks to Leicestershire's Ashby Canal and the Peak Forest Canal at Buxworth to the limestone quarry at Dove Holes. The terminus of the Cromford Canal was extended eastwards into Nottinghamshire by the Pinxton-Mansfield Railway. The most ambitious scheme, however, was begun in 1825 – the year of Stephenson's 'Rocket' – at the Peakland start of this canal: the Cromford and High Peak Railway was a true triumph of engineering, snaking across the White Peak in a series of inclined planes, levels and sharp bends, such as the famous Gotham Turn, for 33 miles between Cromford and the Peak Forest Canal at Whaley Bridge. Stations along it were called wharves but, as always, the waterless limestone terrain had proved to be a determining historic factor, in this case being unsuitable for canals. Jessop's son, Josias, was the engineer and he employed the paternal fish-bellied rails on gritstone sleepers. Of the line's importance, Glover, writing the year before its opening in 1830, was in no doubt: 'The advantages to the district through which it runs will be very great, as it will be supplied with coal at a much lower rate . . . and lime will be rendered much cheaper'. Wagons were horse-drawn along the level stretches and hauled up the inclined planes by ropes attached to stationary steam engines, but from 1841 steam locomotives were used. Passengers had to walk on the inclines.

Also in 1841, Thomas Cook of Melbourne organised his first excursion for steam train passengers. His efforts, an instant success, primarily concerned Leicestershire but soon attracted national demand from which his famous travel firm was founded. Derbyshire's south-eastern neighbour had already influenced the great railway age in his native county when the opening of a line from Leicester to Swannington on the Leicestershire coalfield in 1832 gave rise to too serious competition from the Erewash coalfield in supplying the lucrative south Midlands markets. To keep coal prices suitably low, tolls on the Erewash Canal were reduced at the request of local colliery owners, but before long plans were mooted to build a railway link between the area and Leicester.

The advances in steam-power in the form of locomotive-drawn trains for carrying both passengers and goods marked the beginning of decline in canal trade, despite tolls being cut several times. As carriers such as Pickfords who had introduced a passenger 'fly-boat' service on some Derbyshire canals soon realised, railways had the assets of greater speed and reliability, besides cheap transport costs. Canals frozen over in winter and short of water in summer were occasional hazards causing inevitable delays to their traffic. The Erewash bye-laws stipulated a penalty of £3 in the early 19th century for any boat passing through a

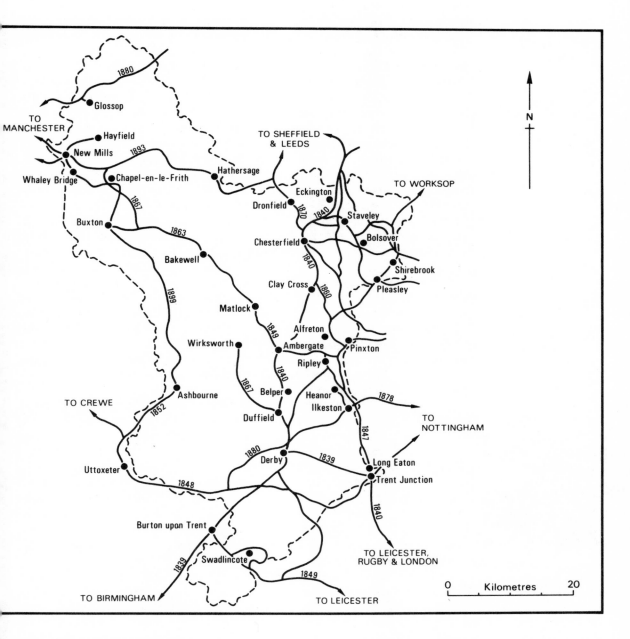

Map 12. Railways after 1839: in the Peak fewer lines, constructed at comparatively later dates, tell a different story for highland and lowland areas, as so often in Derbyshire's history.

lock alone during times of water scarcity, and in 1844 a singularly Derbyshire problem beset the Cromford Canal when lead-mining reached deeper than the level of the Cromford Sough, resulting in so sharp a fall in the canal's water supply that boats with a cargo exceeding only ten tons could not navigate it. Tonnage had totalled 325,000 on this canal in 1828 – 230,000 tons of which was coal – but as railways literally gained ground from 1840-50, Cromford traffic reflected a general trend in shrinking from over 322,000 to 284,700 tons.

Map 12 shows the development of Derbyshire's railways from the first line, Derby-Nottingham, opened in 1839 using trains with engines built at Butterley, to the 1890s when the Sheffield-Manchester route, threading its way through tunnels and along Dark Peak valleys, and the Ashbourne-Buxton, enabling greater access to Dovedale, were opened. Stephenson engineered the North Midland line of 1840 from Derby to Leeds via Ambergate, Clay Cross and Chesterfield, and was aided by his son Robert in laying the Derby-Birmingham line of 1839. This provided the county town with a railway link to London, and the opening of a line from Long Eaton through Leicester and Rugby, also in 1840, added an alternative. In 1856, however, when the nursing heroine Florence Nightingale shunned London publicity after the Crimean War by travelling immediately home to Leahurst, near Matlock, the Derby-Manchester route across the Peak only extended to Rowsley. Not until 1863 was it finally completed, following the Wye valley and including a tunnel behind Haddon Hall plus the five-arched viaduct in Monsal Dale so decried by John Ruskin as a desecration of the landscape, yet nowadays so integral to its beautiful surroundings.

As the focus of important routes, Derby became in 1844 the headquarters of the Midland Railway Company, which established there its own works for building carriages, wagons and locomotives. A prosperous market town was suddenly a major industrial centre. Within its contrasting shire, a chain reaction was set off especially along the eastern coalfield, where amongst the network of railways the main line was from Long Eaton along the Erewash valley, eventually joining the northern line at Clay Cross. The railways brought another new element to Derbyshire's history: urban development. This, in its turn, led to new forms of transport, from horse-drawn tramcars to Rolls-Royces and advanced passenger trains. And yet 19th-century Peakland, so recently independent of packhorse trains, was one of the last places in England to retain road tolls and postal services by stagecoach.

Monsal Dale Viaduct, the subject of a preservation order since 1970

XVI   Towns and City

'Grim, stony and unsheltered' was George Eliot's description of Wirksworth in *Adam Bede*, her novel set at the turn of the 18th century – though she did concede that Ashbourne was a 'pretty town'. Wirksworth, where her aunt Elizabeth Evans was a Methodist preacher, was Derbyshire's fourth largest settlement in 1801, behind Derby, Chesterfield and Belper. But despite its population rising from 2,978 then to 3,807 a century later, such had been the phenomenal expansion of other railway-linked industrial centres, in or near coalfields, that by 1901 Wirksworth ranked close to fortieth.

The following table shows the population growth of today's four largest settlements:

Ashbourne church, 'the finest mere parish church in England' according to George Eliot

	1801	1851	1901	1931	1981
Derby	10,832	40,609	69,266	137,810	214,430
Chesterfield	7,330	13,421	39,955	68,010	68,706
Ilkeston	2,422	6,122	25,384	33,813	32,937
Long Eaton	504	933	13,045	22,339	32,806

Until the railway era, only the boroughs of Derby and Chesterfield were sufficiently populous to count as truly urban, but Ilkeston, still a relatively rural market centre in 1801, achieved borough status in 1887. Long Eaton so outgrew its ancient mother parish of Sawley that in 1934 the latter became part of its urban district. A county population which had increased almost five-fold in 100 years led to the creation of a new diocese of Derby in 1927, with All Saints' church designated as its Cathedral.

Besides Derby, Chesterfield and Ilkeston, only four other places amongst Derbyshire's present urban 'top 20' were medieval market towns: Glossop, Alfreton, Ripley and Bolsover. As with all of these, proximity to railways and/or coalfields – and, for the eastern towns, the M1 motorway – applies to the rest: Heanor, Swadlincote, Dronfield, Buxton, Matlock, Staveley, Belper, Eckington, Shirebrook, Brimington, New Mills and Clay Cross. However, the long existence of the majority of these in Derbyshire's settlement pattern is confirmed by their inclusion in Domesday Book 900 years ago.

Although the county's urban history of the last two centuries essentially reflects national trends, these are diversely interwoven with its

109

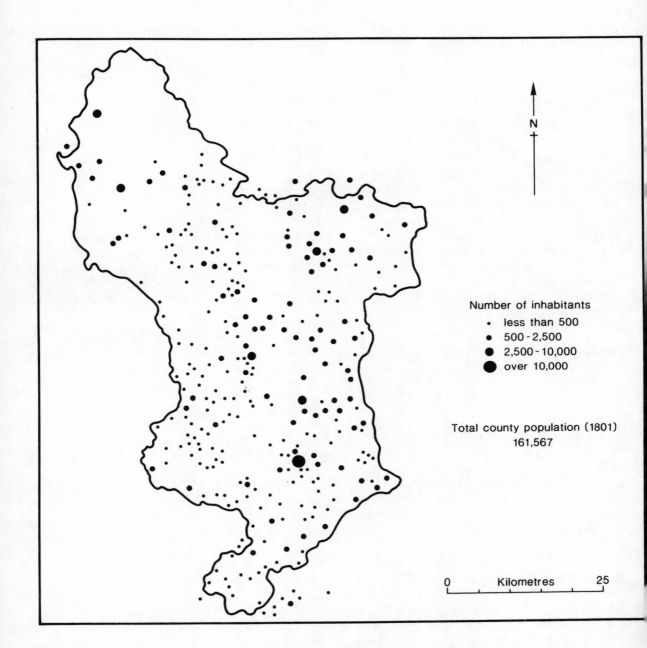

Number of inhabitants

• less than 500

• 500 - 2,500

● 2,500 - 10,000

● over 10,000

Total county population (1801)
161,567

0   Kilometres   25

Map 13. Population distribution at the beginning of the 19th century, a fairly even pattern throughout the county

110

distinctive local flavour. An outstanding 19th-century author such as George Eliot may have had to adopt a male pseudonym to gain greater recognition of her work, but amid Buxton's increasing 20th-century role as a conference centre came a foretaste of the modern feminist movement as early as 1916, when women teachers demonstrated outside the National Union of Teachers' annual gathering, in their campaign for equal pay! Both Buxton, which at an altitude of 1,000 feet became England's highest borough, and Matlock enjoyed their heyday as inland spas in the late 19th and early 20th centuries after the railways brought in many more visitors. At Matlock, John Smedley, a hosiery manufacturer from Lea, introduced the hydropathic 'water cure' in 1853, which attracted noble, famous and foreign patients for treatment. Yet in these times of continuous change, the buildings comprising 'Smedley's Hydro' up steep Matlock Bank nowadays house Derbyshire County Council's headquarters, and Riber Castle, his private residence dominating the town since 1850, is an animal reserve.

Riber Castle

William Howitt's books featuring wildlife and other rural subjects were much influenced by his happy childhood taking 'delicious country walks' around his native Heanor in the 1790s, when it was a village of about one thousand people – his formative years contrasting starkly with those of Ilkeston children labouring long hours in collieries, of whom a mines commissioner reported in 1842 that after work they were 'too tired to play'. Howitt's brother died at Heanor at exactly the same time as the author himself abroad in 1879, but the next available census – 1881 – revealed a population totalling over eleven thousand in Heanor Urban District. Four years later and two miles away, another writer, D. H. Lawrence, was born at Eastwood, just inside Nottinghamshire. Amongst his vivid descriptions of industrial Derbyshire is that beginning his short story, *Tickets Please*, of the green and cream double-decker tramcars hurtling and clattering along the unusually lengthy electric tramway route, which crossed the coal-blighted area between Ripley and Nottingham from 1913-33.

'Dull Derby', as the 19th-century philosopher Herbert Spencer called his birthplace, was not entirely so to visitors who came by rail excursions to see its trendsetting acquisition of 1840: England's first public park, the Arboretum, presented by Josiah Strutt. The changing townscape included the Markeaton Brook being cultivated beneath the centre in 1839, though this did not prevent a memorable April Fool's Day in 1842 when floodwater reached a level of almost five feet, so a commemorative plaque indicates. The level was even higher when the brook flooded in May 1932, but in 1933 Derby Corporation had its course diverted partly by the construction of the lake in Markeaton Park, a scheme which also temporarily created work for unemployed men hit by the Great Depression.

Derby's device of 'the Buck in the Park'

Later in the same decade, when the Munich Agreement narrowly averted World War II in September 1938, celebrations planned at

111

Chesterfield that month for the 250th anniversary of the Glorious Revolution had to be delayed, against the national and international background of uncertainty, until October. Whittington Moor, near Revolution House, was hunting ground when the conspirators of 1688 met there, but in its urban setting of 1938 Corporation motorbuses replaced the trolleybus service which had plied between Chesterfield market place and this suburb since 1927, having then replaced electric tramcars.

Wartime Derby's worst experience occurred on 27 July 1942 when a bombing raid coincided with the morning and night shifts changing over at Rolls-Royce's main works in Nightingale Road. Of the sixty or so casualties, 22 people were killed. In 1946 the company, having specialised in aero engines as well as cars for most of its 30-year existence in Derby, turned its immense capacity entirely over to the former by transferring car production to its works at Crewe. Derby's industrial expansion is owed not only to the railways and its choice in 1906 as the headquarters of Rolls-Royce but has been strongly based too on the establishment of other major firms a such as Qualcast, near the railways, and Courtaulds-Celanese (formerly British Celanese). Although additionally it became the headquarters of Trent Motor Traction Company, begun in 1913 (now part of the National Bus Company), the development of public transport services within the spreading borough originated as another railway influence. For after trains started steaming into Friar Gate Station on the Great Northern Railway's Derbyshire Extension line from Nottingham, opened in 1878, horse-drawn buses provided a link between this and the Midland Railway Station. The horses were stabled near Friar Gate Railway Bridge, and tramlines still exist in the cobbled yard of the old transport depot there, recalling that horse trams operated from 1880-1907. Derby Corporation introduced electric trams in 1904, which began to be replaced by trolleybuses from January 1932 and these ran until September 1967. The conversion of routes to motorbuses, however, began five years earlier along the Nottingham Road.

Ilkeston's industrial archaeology includes the power station erected in 1902 to provide electricity for the town's trams which began service in 1903, a year ahead of Derby and also Chesterfield (where horse-drawn trams were used from 1882). Besides coal, which reached its highest production after the railway boom, a contributory factor to the growth of Ilkeston, Long Eaton and Heanor in particular was the extension of the factory system, using steam-power, to their home-based textile trades of hosiery and its offshoot, lace, in the mid-19th century. A great subsequent increase in output benefited the industries' workers too, with shorter hours and higher wages. Some 19th-century lace factories, for example the Albion Works dating from 1845 at Ilkeston, have been in unbroken use, despite a recent decline in lace manufacture; others are now associated with a range of newer industries, such as upholstery, electrical goods and plastics.

47. (*above*) Derwent church spire, rising out of the Ladybower Reservoir a year after the latter's opening by King George VI in 1945, stood as a monument to the submerged villages of Derwent and Ashopton, but was demolished in December 1947, having been deemed a safety hazard. The vicarage was also demolished after the death of the village's last vicar.

48. (*right*) Derwent Reservoir and Dam: completed during the First World War, it formed the practice zone for the famous Dam Busters of the Second.

49. (*above left*) Memorial to Tip, 'the most devoted sheepdog in history', near Derwent Dam. Tip was found alive, but emaciated, after keeping vigil by the body of her master on Howden Moor for 15 weeks in the severe winter of 1953-4, and died the winter after her ordeal. Her story attracted subscriptions worldwide for this memorial.

50. (*above right*) Elvaston Castle, acquired by the Derbyshire County Council in 1969, along with a 200-acre estate which was opened as the county's first country park in 1970. The castle, dating from 1817, was once the home of the Stanhope family, lords of Elvaston from the 16th century, and earls of Harrington from the 18th. The country park contains a working museum which reconstructs life on a great estate around 1910.

51. Dovedale.

52. (*above left*) Hope Valley Cement Works (with the 'shivering' face of Mam Tor behind), is a dominant landscape feature within the Peak National Park boundaries, but was built in 1929, long before the Park existed. It provides employment for several hundred local inhabitants.

53. (*above right*) Limestone quarrying in the enclave around Buxton which was specifically excluded from the National Park for mineral extraction. About 70 per cent of the White Peak output of limestone is used in road-building or concrete, and most of the remainder for cement making.

54. Odin lead mine, Castleton.

55. (*left*) Walkers approaching Rushup Edge above Edale.

56. (*below*) View from Kinder Downfall on Kinderscout.

'Hilly Holies', also at Ilkeston, is a local name for one of the many former mining sites in the eastern coalfield today. The attraction of modern, light industries especially to its southern portion around Ilkeston, Heanor, Ripley and Alfreton has helped to offset the impact of colliery closures in the 1960s and '70s, as coal seams became finally worked out. Industrial estates have proliferated within easy reach of the M1, some on defunct colliery sites. Late 20th-century society's emphasis on leisure pursuits has led, however, to the reclamation of several disused workings as recreation grounds, playing fields and open spaces such as the country park at Shipley outlined in Chapter XVII.

A Derbyshire industrial town particularly well-served by pleasant walks is Belper, which also became an important centre for hosiery after the advent of steam-power into textile industries, its population growing steadily from 4,500 in 1801 to almost 16,500 in 1981. Lower down the Derwent valley, the Evans family's early cotton manufacturing village at Darley Abbey expanded to form a substantial Derby suburb and was amongst several formerly separate villages incorporated within the borough boundary in 1968. Others included Allestree, Alvaston, Chellaston, Littleover, Mickleover and Spondon.

Local government reorganisation in April 1974 involved the merging of Derby borough and Derbyshire under one education authority and the creation of new administrative districts to supersede urban and rural district councils, which resulted in the following divisions, in addition to Derby and Chesterfield: Amber Valley, Bolsover, Erewash, High Peak, North-East Derbyshire, South Derbyshire and West Derbyshire. Derby itself was finally elevated to city status in July 1977, the distinction being marked by a visit from Her Majesty the Queen during her Silver Jubilee celebrations. The former borough had, however, begun the decade with another momentous event: the sudden collapse of Rolls-Royce on 4 February 1971, a great shock both to its workforce and the people of Derby in general. Rolls-Royce (1971) Ltd., set up in its place, took time to re-establish success but achieved this so remarkably that in the mid-1980s the company secured, against international competition, the largest order for aero engines yet known in civil aviation history. During the industrial uncertain of the early 1970s which followed Rolls-Royce's fall, a welcome morale booster was brought to many Derbeians by the local professional football club, Derby County, twice winning the League Championship, before later experiencing fluctuating fortunes.

Inner-city development in recent times has seen major changes take place, for instance in the redirection of traffic flow and creation of pedestrian shopping areas and a new theatre. The demolition of Derby's Victorian Midland Railway Station for a modern successor aroused much controversy, especially in view of the fact that 19th-century buildings in its immediate surroundings intrinsic to the city's railway heritage have been restored. Indeed, heritage and conservation have

Medieval 'Headless Cross', Friar Gate, Derby

113

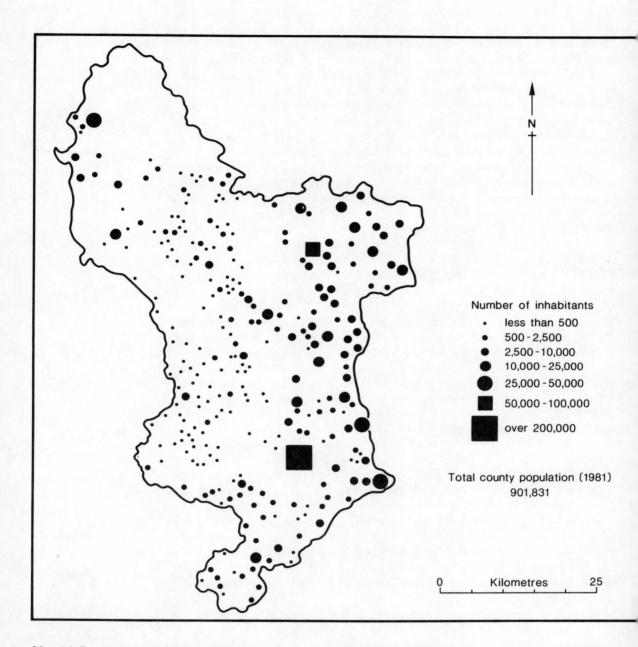

Map 14. Population distribution in 1981: in the west, the pattern has remained much the same as in 1801, but the east shows the massive concentration resulting from 19th- and 20th-century industrialisation. The estimated population figure for 1984 suggested an increase of almost 10,000 over the 1981 figures.

114

become key words in the modern era: Chesterfield has its Peacock Heritage Centre in an early Tudor timber-framed house which has survived, and Derby its Friar Gate Conservation Area. Here, however, the decorative iron Railway Bridge has faced possible demolition to make room for a further stage of the Inner Ring Road, and may require modification to strengthen it amid the transport revolution which has continued through the far greater use of motor-cars and lorries in the latter half of the 20th century, linking town, city and countryside. To the Derbyshire countryside, already much pressurised by the needs of large urban centres both inside and outside the county – whether for leisure purposes, water supplies from the Dark Peak or electricity from the coal-fired power stations along the Trent valley – the heavier volume of road traffic has brought advantages and disadvantages. But heritage and conservation in a rural context are intermingled with the positive and resilient response of Derbyshire's greatest natural resource to the period of intensive industrialisation – the asset to which the final chapter of this book is devoted: its outstanding beauty.

Old Glossop, the Peak District's largest town

XVII Countryside

Victoria Diamond Jubilee Memorial in its White Peak setting at Bradbourne

If Daniel Defoe could return nowadays to the Peak District he described as 'wild and abandoned' in 1725, he would find many parts still wild – but protected, amid powerful and continuing conflicts of interest. And doubtless Lord Byron would still reiterate his early 19th-century statement, mentioned in the Preface, about Derbyshire's scenic attractiveness. While the county population has edged ever nearer to a million since his day, however, that of the industrial towns and cities within a 60-mile radius of Peakland has collectively swelled to about eighteen million and the very solitude of the upland's open spaces has made it an obvious place of temporary escape from urban environments, its higher rainfall an obvious catchment area to satisfy their vast needs for water and its mineral wealth the major national source of limestone for road-building. The necessity for equilibrium between these demands, Peakland agriculture, the interests of people living and working within the region and preservation of a landscape so valuable for education as well as recreation made the Peak District National Park the obvious choice too as the forerunner of Britain's 10 such areas when it came into being on 17 April 1951, funded mostly by government grants and about half the remainder by Derbyshire, into which the greatest proportion of its 542 square miles extends. The only National Park managed by its own independent board, based at Bakewell, its solutions to conservation problems in the county have often been imaginative, its tasks often considerable.

The special qualities of the Derbyshire Peak have been enhanced by a resurgence of customs in the 19th and 20th centuries: ancient, annual and new. Although, as noted in Chapter XII, some customs were no more after the early industrial period, others – especially well-dressing – were begun or revived in many places as the Victorian era wore on. In most customs, whether stalwart survivors such as Tissington's celebrated festival or 20th-century innovations such as the Padley pilgrimages, religious links have endured strongly. Their popularity with urban visitors has perhaps partly ensured their continuance. A deeper and wider appreciation of the county's customs, traditions and folklore is perceptible from about the 1820s. One of many literary forms through which this found expression was an early-established historical journal called *The Reliquary* edited by the local antiquarian, Llewellyn Jewitt. Archaeology featured also in its contents, which – though general –

concentrated mainly on Derbyshire. In volume 10 (1870), Jewitt published his synopsis for a county history which he never completed. In 1878, however, the Derbyshire Archaeological Society was founded and has produced the county archaeological journal since the following year.

*Turreted tower on
the Derwent Dam*

Unusually, Derbyshire lead-mining is one activity whose customs have lived on, while the industry itself has largely disappeared. An indirect outcome of its decline was the erection of a cotton mill on the site of demolished smeltworks at the Cromford end of Via Gellia, which was purchased by W. H. Collins of Pleasley Mill in 1890: a few years later, the road's local appellation 'Vi Jella', apparently inspired the company's well-known 'Viyella' trademark for its blended wool and cotton fabric, still produced at Somercotes. 'Jumbo', 'Alice' and 'Baby' were the three Cornish pumping engines at Millclose Mine, Darley Dale, which paradoxically became the richest individual mine in Derbyshire's history as lead-mining generally ceased. Veins of ore discovered after its reopening in the 1860s produced 500,000 tons from then until its final demise in 1939, accounting for most of Britain's output between the wars. Constant flooding problems and consequently high pumping costs (5,000 gallons per minute had to be discharged by 1938!) caused its closure. Old lead-mining drainage soughs now contribute to urban water drawn from the Peak – Meerbrook Sough at Wirksworth, for example, began supplying Heanor and Ilkeston around 1908.

The Dark Peak's propensity to retain surface water has engendered frequent, light-hearted allusions to the Peakland 'Lake District' due to its many man-made reservoirs, in addition to some reputedly haunted natural pools. Depopulation of several agricultural communities occurred as the livelihoods of a few lost out to a basic requirement of millions, when reservoirs were created in the main river valleys: along the Etherow in Longdendale between 1848 and 1875, and in the Goyt and upper Derwent valleys in the 1930s. On the banks of Ladybower overlooking where the former villages of Derwent and Ashopton stood, a sense of sadness lingers. During severe droughts, such as in summer 1976, this has acquired visual form when the ruins of cottages, churches and 17th-century Derwent Hall, once a popular youth hostel, reappeared. Upstream, Howden Dam was completed in 1912 as the first authorised under the Derwent Valley Water Act of 1899. Derwent Dam followed in 1916 and when the 'Dam Busters' practised on these before their memorable World War II raid on Germany, the Ladybower Dam was well under construction. Since its million tons of earth and 100,000 tons each of concrete and clay allowed the opening of Ladybower Reservoir in 1945, the upper Derwent valley has taken on an almost Alpine beauty as the moorlands rise above hillsides of conifers planted during the 20th century. Like the narrow Goyt valley which was endangered until 1970 by the sheer numbers of visitors attracted by car, the area has a traffic-free scheme introduced by the National Park

Tissington Trail

authority to operate at summer weekends and bank holidays, with minibus services for non-pedestrians.

An early success for the Peak Park board was the negotiation of agreements allowing public access to the high moors, apart from on a few days each year during the grouse-shooting season (12 August-10 December). Before 1951, these areas were strictly private game reserves which had witnessed many clashes between ramblers and gamekeepers. Park Hall Moor, the scene of conflict during the famous Mass Trespass on 24 April 1932 when some six hundred ramblers approached Kinder Scout from Hayfield, was added to the National Trust's Derbyshire property in 1986, Kinder itself having been acquired by the Trust in 1982. The access movements spawned during the hardship of the Great Depression included the idea of Britain's first long-distance footpath, the Pennine Way, put forward by the journalist Tom Stephenson in 1935. Thirty years elapsed before its complete realisation along the 250 miles from Edale across Kinder, Bleaklow and Black Hill to the Scottish border. Nowadays, the main battle concerning the route is against erosion, particularly where thousands of boots tread near its popular start!

Government and EEC grants are available to farmers in the National Park, for example to repair dry-stone walls. But unlike overseas counterparts which are mostly state-owned, approximately seventy per cent. of the Peak Park is still privately owned, the remainder belonging to water and local authorities, the National Trust, Forestry Commission and about five per cent. actually to the Park board. Disused Peakland railway lines bought after closures in the late 1960s and converted to walking, cycling and nature trails form part of this in Derbyshire: the Cromford and High Peak Railway became the High Peak Trail; much of the Ashbourne-Buxton line, the Tissington Trail; and Bakewell-Buxton, the Monsal Trail.

Near the latter's Wyedale start, Topley Pike limestone quarry, which is just inside the Park, was refused permission in May 1986 for a 19-acre expansion. Such an occurrence underlines the complexity of striking a balance between conservation and the often incompatible needs of industry. More than two-thirds of Derbyshire's limestone is produced outside the Park boundary – mostly from the enclave around Buxton (shown on Map 15) which includes Europe's largest quarry at Tunstead. But an annual output of around four million tons inside the Park makes quarrying important for local employment. Lorries trundling through Peakland villages and along narrow, steep and winding roads to transport the stone are conjectured at seven hundred per day. As with limestone, Derbyshire is Britain's greatest source of fluorspar, producing over four-fifths of the national total for wide-ranging chemical use. Most is obtained inside the Peak Park from opencast and underground mines, or waste hillocks bequeathed by lead-mining. A problematic legacy of fluorspar mining is the disposal of its own considerable waste, which

118

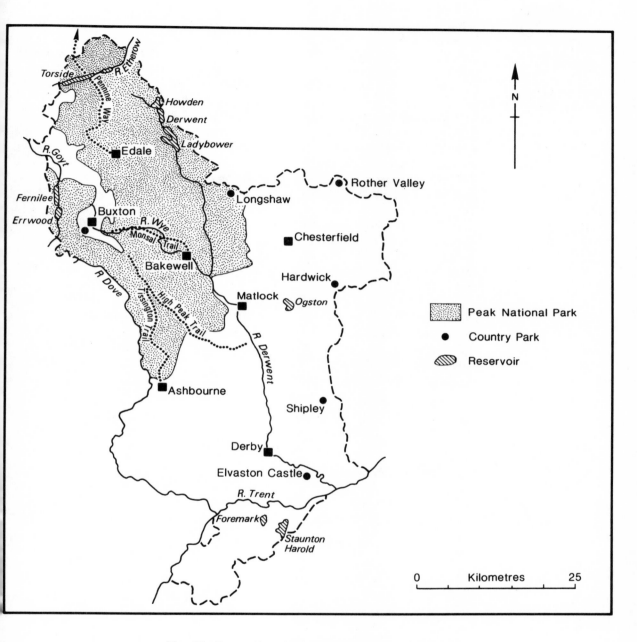

Map 15. Innovations in the Derbyshire countryside.

119

Solomon's Temple,
Buxton Country Park

will be a continuing reality in landscape rescue work for time to come. Schemes currently in progress include some sealing of dangerous old lead   mineshafts.

As noted in Chapter XVI, improving extractive industrial sites has also entailed much effort in lowland Derbyshire. Shipley Country Park contains the site of an old opencast colliery transformed to complement the grounds of the former Shipley Hall. Since Elvaston Castle and 200-acre grounds became Derbyshire's first country park in 1970, other one-time preserves of the privileged have been created into similar havens to help offset urban pressures. Longshaw Country Park, near Sheffield, for example, formerly belonged to the Dukes of Rutland for shooting.

The break-up of great estates under hefty 20th-century taxation has passed much property into protected ownership for public amenity. Increasingly in the post-war years, the National Trust's work has embraced not only unspoilt scenery such as Longshaw, Dovedale and Kinder in the Peak Park but the architectural heritage of Hardwick, Sudbury and, more recently, Calke Abbey, whose reclusive Harpur Crewe owners seem to have been far less gregarious than the canons of the medieval priory on which the great house stands. In Derbyshire's ongoing story, the future of Kedleston Hall also appears assured. But amid the timeless essence of Derbyshire's highland-lowland divide, the picture of this historic county's past inevitably remains incomplete and future studies may well modify and enrich our present understanding of what Llewellyn Jewitt so fittingly called 'one of the most favoured and important counties within the confines of the kingdom'.

Select Bibliography

The abbreviation *DAJ* refers to the *Derbyshire Archaeological Journal*.

Andrews, M., *Long Ago in Peakland*, 9th edn. (1976).

Andrews, W. (ed.), *Bygone Derbyshire* (1892).

Bateman, T., *Vestiges of the Antiquities of Derbyshire* (1848); *Ten Years' Diggings* (1861).

Bramwell, D., *Archaeology in the Peak District* (1973).

Coates, E., 'The Origin and Distribution of Fairs in Medieval Derbyshire', *DAJ*, vol. 85 (1965).

Colvin, H., *Calke Abbey, Derbyshire: a Hidden House Revealed* (1985).

Cox, J. C., *Churches of Derbyshire*, vols. 1-4 (1875).

Derbyshire Archaeological Society, *Derbyshire Industrial Archaeology: a Gazetteer*, Parts 1 and 2 (1986).

Dodd, A. E. and E. M., *Peakland Roads and Trackways*, 2nd edn. (1980).

Durant, D. N., *Bess of Hardwick* (1977).

Edmunds, W. H., *Wingfield Manor* (undated).

Farey, J., *General View of the Agriculture and Minerals of Derbyshire*, vols. 1-3 (1811, 1813, 1817).

Fraser, A., *Mary Queen of Scots* (1969).

Garlick, T., *Roman Derbyshire* (1974).

Glover, S., *History of Derbyshire* (1829).

Green, H., 'The Southern Portion of the Nottinghamshire and Derbyshire Coalfield and the Development of Transport before 1850', *DAJ*, vol. 56 (1935).

Hall, I., *Georgian Buxton* (1984).

Hallam, V. J., *Silent Valley* (1983).

Hart, C. R., *North Derbyshire Archaeological Survey to A.D. 1500* (1981).

Heath, J. E., *History of Derbyshire* (1982).

Higgens, C. W., 'The Framework Knitters of Derbyshire', *DAJ*, vol. 71 (1951).

Hopkinson, G. G., 'The Inland Navigations of the Derbyshire and Nottinghamshire Coalfield 1777-1856', *DAJ*, vol. 79 (1959).

Hutton, W., *History of Derby* (1791).

Jenkinson, R. D. S., *British Archaeological Reports, No. 122 'Creswell Crags: Late Pleistocene Sites in the East Midlands'* (1984).

Jewitt, L., *Stately Homes of England* (1874).

Kaye, D., *British Bus Fleets: East Midlands* (1965).

Kitching, J. W., *Bone, Tooth and Horn Tools of Palaeolithic Man* (1963).

Morris, J. (ed.), *Domesday Book: Derbyshire* (1978).

Page, W. (ed.), *Victoria County History of Derbyshire*, vols. 1-2 (1905-7).

Parker, H. M. and Willies, L., *Peakland Lead Mines and Miners* (1979).

Rodgers, F., *Derby Old and New*, 3rd edn. (1984).

Roffe, D., *The Derbyshire Domesday* (1986).

Sheffield City Libraries, *Dorothy Vernon's Elopement: Tale or Tradition?* (1960).

Smith, G. le Blanc, *Haddon, the Hall, the Manor, its Lords and Traditions* (1906).

Smith, R., *First and Last: the Peak National Park* (1978).

Stallybrass, B., 'Bess of Hardwick's Buildings and Building Accounts', *Archaeologia*, vol. 64 (1913).

Unwin, G., *Samuel Oldknow and the Arkwrights* (1924).

Wainwright, F. T., 'Early Scandinavian Settlement in Derbyshire', *DAJ*, vol. 67 (1947).

Warrender, K., *High Peak Faces and Places* (1978).

Whitaker, P. D., *Early Settlement in Derbyshire* (1974).

Index

124

126

Powtrell family, 77, 81
Pursglove, Bishop Robert, 73, 74, 75, 77

Quakers, 81
quarrying, 89, 93, 106, 116, 118

Radbourne, 82
railways, 106, 108, 109, 111, 112; decline,
  113, 114, 118
Ravencliffe cave, 18
Repton, 36-7, 39, 41, 42, 45-6; priory, 55, 57,
  58, 59-60; school, 72, 73-4, 75
Repton and Gresley Hundred, 43
Revolution House, 81, 111
Rhodes: Ebenezer, 22; Francis, 75
Riber castle, 111
Ringham Low, 25
Ripley, 92, 99, 109, 111, 113
Risley, 73, 75
Robin Hood, 47, 87
Robin Hood's cave, 20, 47; Stride, 27, 47
Rolleston, George, 77
Rolls Royce, 101, 111, 113
Roosdyche, 30
Rowsley, 36, 108
Rowter Rocks, 26
Roystone Grange, 33, 34, 52
Rutland, 9th Earl, 86; dukes and earls of,
  90, 102, 120; *see also* Manners
Ryknield Street, 42

Sacheverell family, 77
St Helen's chantry, Chesterfield, 73
St Helen's priory, Derby, 57
St James's priory, 59
St Leonard's Hospital, 57
St Loe, Sir William, 69
St Mary's bridge, 53, 93
St Mary's priory, 59
Sandiacre, 52, 104
Savage family, 61, 62
Sawley, 39, 104, 109
Scarcliffe, 34, 84
Seward, Anna, 88
Shardlow, 102, 103
Sheldon, 83
Sherwood Forest, 50
Shipley, 92, 104, 113, 120
Shirebrook, 34, 109
Shottle, 33
Shrewsbury: Elizabeth, Countess of, (Bess
  of Hardwick), 68-71, 72, 77, 78; 2nd Earl
  of, 68; 4th Earl of, 68; George, 6th Earl
  of, 67-8, 69-70, 77-9; 7th Earl of, 86
Smalley, 92

Smedley, John, 111
Smisby, 42
Smythson, Robert, 70
Snake Pass, 103
Somercotes, 92, 117
Somersal Herbert, 62
South Normanton, 92, 96
South Wingfield, 68, 99
Spencer, Herbert, 111
Spend Lane, 63
Spondon, 39, 113
Stainsby, 42
Stanhope, Sir John, 80
Stanley: Sir Thomas, 67, 77; Rev. Thomas, 88
Stanley Park, 58
Stanton-by-Bridge, 47
Stanton Moor, 22, 25, 26-7, 90
Stathum, John, 59
Staveley, 92, 93, 104, 109; school, 73, 75
Steetley, 54
Stephenson, George, 101, 104, 106, 108;
  Tom, 118
Stoney Low, 21, 25
Stoney Middleton, 79, 84
Street, The, (Roman road), 30, 31, 33, 34,
  35
Strutt: Jedediah, 96; Josiah, 111; family, 98-
  9, 102
Strutt's Park, 31
Stuart: Lady Arabella, 70, 71, 72, 78; Prince
  Charles Edward, 82
Sudbury, 85-6, 120
Swadlincote, 109
Swanwick, 92, 99
Swarkestone, 80, 82, 104

Taddington, 74
Talbot family, *see* Shrewsbury, earls of
Thacker, Gilbert, 60, 73
Thirst House, cave, 23
Thorpe, 43, 63, 103
Ticknall, 93, 106
Tideswell, 48, 52, 54, 86; school, 73, 74, 75
Tissington, 61-4, 80, 84, 87, 103, 116; Trail,
  118
Topley Pike, 118
Torside, 31
tramways, 101, 104, 106, 111, 112
Trent river, 18, 103, 104; valley, 23, 29, 36
Trent and Mersey Canal, 103, 104
Trowell, 104
Trusley, 83
Tunstead, 103, 118
turnpikes, 102-3, 104

Unstone, 93